HD
6475
.A1
W44

Weinberg, Paul.

European labor and
multinationals

HD
6475
.A1
W44

Weinberg, Paul.

European labor and
multinationals

cop.2

18.95

| DATE | BORROWER'S NAME | |
|------|-----------------|---|
| | | |
| | | |
| | | |
| | | |
| | | |

# EUROPEAN LABOR AND MULTINATIONALS

# EUROPEAN LABOR AND MULTINATIONALS

## PAUL J. WEINBERG

**PRAEGER PUBLISHERS**
**Praeger Special Studies**

New York • London • Sydney • Toronto

**Library of Congress Cataloging in Publication Data**

Weinberg, Paul.
  European labor and multinationals.

  Bibliography: p. 102
  1. International labor activities. 2. Trade-
unions—Europe. 3. International business
enterprises. I. Title.
HD6475.A1W44 1978    331.88'091    78-9449

ISBN 0-03-044256-7

PRAEGER SPECIAL STUDIES
383 Madison Avenue, New York, N.Y., 10017, U.S.A.

Published in the United States of America in 1978
by Praeger Publishers,
A Division of Holt, Rinehart and Winston, CBS, Inc.

89 038 987654321

# CONTENTS

vi

# LIST OF TABLES AND FIGURE

# EUROPEAN LABOR AND MULTINATIONALS

# INTRODUCTION

This is a study about the representatives of workers—trade unions —and how they have responded to the growth of multinational corporations (MNCs). International labor action is an old idea and, of course, espoused by Karl Marx. Multinational corporate entities have existed in various forms, even prior to the industrial revolution. However, only since World War II have they come to be transnational economic centers with a type of power heretofore attributable only to the nation-state.

Trade unions have responded to this new distribution of power. Efforts by them to get "more," to use the adage of Samuel Gompers, have resulted in the development of a multinational corporate strategy that transcends traditional state boundaries. This research explores how this strategy is constituted and what the implications are for political science. Most particularly, is the state-centric paradigm of political science an outdated concept?

Concurrent with the rise of MNCs has been the development of economic regionalism, most notably the European Economic Community (EEC). Europe is thus an ideal "laboratory" for the study of transnational labor action because it is a highly integrated economic area; it is one of the three centers of MNC decision making, the others being the United States and Japan; and it has a long history of well-developed "free" trade unions.

Economic integration coupled with the growth of the multinational corporation in the developed world, particularly in Western Europe, has been on the ascendancy since World War II. The development of the EEC as well as the growth of multinationals in basic industry has encouraged a sense of mutual economic interdependency throughout Europe. Although the original long-range objectives of Monet, Schu-

1

man and Henri-Spaak for European political integration appear to have been thwarted, the motivating force of economic integration has created a body politic that has a sense of self-interest beyond national borders.

H. Stephenson, the noted British financial expert, has stated, "Between 1958 and 1963 American companies established or bought no fewer than 3,000 subsidiaries in EEC countries. Italy's estimates are that one in four of the country's large companies are owned by foreigners, with half of those Americans."[1] The result of this trend is that major economic decisions no longer appear to be made in the interest of a particular nation. An argument could be made (which I support) that decisions are made in the name of a corporate interest that frequently owes no allegiance to any state.

The impact of multinational corporate growth on national economies has been noted in numerous works.[2] However, few studies have reviewed the impact and response on and by organized labor in Europe. The importance of workers to MNC growth is noted by R. J. Barnet and R. E. Muller: "The essential strategy of the global corporation is based on the international division of labor."[3] Let us for the moment accept Barnet and Muller's concept that labor strategy is at the core of multinational development. It is therefore crucial to examine the success of this objective. This can be done by looking at the economic integration of the world's economy, MNC growth, and structured regionalism, that is, the EEC. Questions can then be raised about the impact of these developments upon organized labor. Has labor been able to develop transnational coordination and cooperation in Europe? Are trade unions an effective transnational interest group for the maximization of power, particularly against the global MNC strategy of the "international division of labor?" These questions are of central concern to this study and the conclusion will attempt to answer them based upon collected data.

The lesser developed, or third world, countries were specifically not chosen for study because generally, these trade unions are at a more rudimentary stage, either struggling for recognition or basic economic goals, and are frequently tied directly to government; they are remote from MNC decision making; the area is vast and not well integrated, although there are regional exceptions, such as the Organization of Petroleum Exporting Countries (OPEC) and the Latin American Free Trade Association (LAFTA). Marxists may take issue with this approach by viewing the third world as "victim," the object of MNC exploitation.[4] However, it is precisely because of their level of development that they do not yet view transnational labor strategy as a priority —and thus the third world is not suitable for this study.

Canada has been excluded primarily because most labor and MNC integration is with the United States and has been documented by John Crispo.[5] Australia, primarily because of geographic remoteness and lack of significant international labor links, has also been excluded. Furthermore, there are few Australian MNCs with large employee populations outside that country.

This leaves the United States as the final major country to be excluded. The United States is paramount as an economic power, even though it is now being challenged by an integrated Europe. Its labor movement has chosen to forge its international links primarily with Canada, to some extent with Latin America (through the AFL-CIO's American Institute for Latin Development, which has been accused of being CIA funded), and to some degree with Western Europe. However, the focus in the United States has not been on international action.

The AFL-CIO has pressed the United States to withdraw from the International Labor Organization (ILO) and itself dissociated from the International Confederation of Free Trade Unions. Though some U.S. unions have pursued international ties, such as the International Association of Machinists and the United Autoworkers, the impact of this upon transnational labor relations cannot be assessed with full justice within the confines of a single study. Thus Western Europe was chosen, partially for expediency (there is documentation of transnational action) and partially because the area presents an ideal "laboratory" for such research.

In order to assess the extent of transnational labor cooperation between labor unions and vis-a-vis the multinational I have had to develop my own methodology and framework for research. This is primarily due to the paucity of literature in the area and the lack of an existing acceptable framework. The less than exhaustive academic explorations of the relationship between trade unions and multinationals are indicative of the need for research on transnational labor action. The transnationality of organized labor is frequently relegated to a minor position in the context of the "social responsibility" of the MNC or specific economic developments, such as transfer pricing. Even within Barnet and Muller's study of globalization, international labor is relegated to a chapter on "The Obsolescence of American Labor."[6]

Various views of MNCs are held by what I have called the Marxist, "liberal-functionalist," and "minor impact" schools. Each of these ask different questions about labor's relationship to the MNC and these are explored more fully in Chapter 1. It should be noted now that the consequences of Barnet and Muller's concept that the international division of labor is at the core of MNC strategy vary with each school.

To the Marxist, the result is a more effective means of exploitation of labor, and the focus of analysis would be the utilization of local market conditions in relation to home-based industry. The liberal-functionalist would take a more benign view. It is not the intent of this work to support either of the schools, only to determine the extent of transnational labor action and its impact upon political integration.

The need for this research is apparent when one examines the extent of documentation of transnational labor action and cooperation by trade unions with specific respect to the MNC. The literature generally notes the activities of five international trade secretariats that have been extremely active, particularly within the specific industry seen as their organizing sphere. International trade secretariats (ITSs) are central or peak trade union bodies organized on an industrywide basis. Membership is limited to the central national trade union of an industry in each country. Thus the International Metalworkers Federation is represented in the United States by the United Autoworkers. These primarily Geneva-based bodies have been the focal point of academic and "partisan" literature. The International Chemical Workers Federation (ICF) headed by Charles Levinson, and the International Metalworkers Federation (IMF) have been the most vocal on the subject of the multinational. Their efforts have also been the most documented.

Expanded transnational action has important political implications. Potential shifts in loyalty from the nation-state to trade union organizations or other transnational bodies may diminish state sovereignty. Concentrations of power beyond the nation-state to countervail MNC growth may have unplanned and unforeseen economic effects. The lack of research in this area is therefore cause for concern. The potential for research in other areas may also result from this study, for once it is demonstrated that worker activity is focused beyond the nation-state, new notions of power must be addressed that are no longer state-centric.

Because there are only a few reported instances of transnational labor action directed against a specific multinational, none of which can be considered international collective bargaining in the U.S. sense, there has been a tendency to view this as an indication of trade union weakness. This view is not held here. It is the opinion of this author that once one sees the totality of the strategy of trade unions, a new and startling image of trade union power emerges. It is the totality of the strategy this study addresses. As shall be seen in later chapters, the MNC has become a catalyst for present and incipient transnational worker action.

# NOTES

1. H. Stephenson, *The Coming Clash—The Impact of Multinational Corporations on National States* (New York: Saturday Press Review, 1972).

2. Christopher Tugendhat, *The Multinationals* (Middlesex, England: Penguin Books, 1973), R. J. Barnet and R. E. Muller, *Global Reach—The Power of the Multinational Corporations* (New York: Simon & Schuster, 1974); Stephenson, *The Coming Clash;* Charles Kindleberger, *American Business Abroad: Six Lectures on Direct Investments* (New Haven, Conn.: Yale University Press, 1969).

3. Barnet and Muller, *Global Reach,* p. 29; Charles Levinson, *Industry's Democratic Revolution* (London: Allen & Unwin, 1974); Robert W. Cox, "Labor and Transnational Relations," in *Transnational Relations in World Politics,* ed. Robert O. Koehane and Joseph S. Nye (Cambridge, Mass.: Harvard University Press, 1972), pp. 204–34. Other observers, particularly those in the "minor impact" school (to be discussed in Chapter 1) view the role of labor as less crucial. Responsible opinion is that there is a great variation among MNCs on this question and it is generally a function of MNC intensity.

4. There is evidence that tends to refute the Marxist exploitation argument. *Business International* summarizes the article "ILO Gives MNC's High Marks for Wage Work Policies" in the ILO report *Wages and Working Conditions in MNE's,* 3/11/77, p. 78: "In developed countries, international firms generally adapt their wages to local levels ... second, in developing countries ... the average level of employee earnings in international companies far exceeds those in local firms. The difference is often dramatic (usually more than 50%) and seems to be related to the stage of economic development of the country."

5. John Crispo, *International Unionism: A Study in Canadian-American Relations* (Toronto: McGraw-Hill, 1967).

6. Barnet and Muller, *Global Reach.*

# 1 ESTABLISHING A CONCEPTUAL FRAMEWORK: the relevance of current literature to the study of transnational labor relations

The literature treating the multinational is concerned with the effect of that phenomenon upon global economics, frequently with secondary attention to the impact on labor and any subsequent response. Perspectives on the multinational as an integrating force offer insight into various values implicit in research and factors that must be considered when exploring labor as a transnational group. The literature of integration theory is useful for closing conceptual gaps and placing empirical data about an economic interest group into the wider context of transnational political behavior. Furthermore, labor-management relations is looked upon as a key area for future research in the political integration literature. (See note 1 for a list of relevant political integration literature.) Both of these bodies of literature will now be explored as a framework for the study of transnational labor relations in the developed world, particularly Western Europe.

## POLITICAL INTEGRATION LITERATURE

Political scientists have long been active in the study of integration, but the greatest impetus to research was the formation of the EEC. To date, both theory and empirical investigation have been primarily Euro- and state-centric, although there is a growing literature on Latin America and, to a lesser extent, on African economic cooperative efforts.[1] It is in Europe, however, where there has been the greatest movement toward political integration, such as European Coal and Steel Community, Euratom, and the European Parliament. This chapter is concerned with exploring current conceptual frameworks and trends, particularly with a view to the applicability of non-state-centric

6

transnational research. Euro-centered research is therefore a by-product of efforts in this vast area to create and expand various types of regional efforts.

### Conceptual Frameworks: An Overview

Pioneering research in political integration can be attributed to both Ernst Haas[2] and Karl Deutsch.[3] Indeed, most political scientists doing research in this area are intellectual disciples of these two scholars.

Haas delineates schools of integration analysis as the following:

1. Federalism, which is concerned with institutional and constitutional questions. Carl J. Friedrich states, "Federalism is ... understood if it is seen as a process. The main question is: What function does a federal relationship have?—rather than: What structure?"[4] Federalism will not be discussed, as it has been superseded by other approaches and no significant research is being done using this framework.

2. Communications theory, which has a basic tenet that an intensive pattern of communication between national units will result in a closer community if "loads and capabilities remain in balance." Actors are "units," which are equivalent to nations, and groups or people are "incidental." Methodologically theorists are concerned with aggregate and survey data. The "volume of transactions" is a major indicator of political integration and all variables have equal weight. Deutsch is the founder of the communications school.[5]

3. Neofunctionalism traces its roots to David Mitrany.[6] Conclusions are drawn from "case studies of integrative efforts." Joseph Nye,[7] Amatai Etzioni,[8] Haas,[9] L. Lindberg,[10] and S. A. Scheingold[11] are leading neofunctionalists. They stress the incremental effects of nation-states or "actors" and view the consequences of interest groups, political parties, and so on upon political integration. Great faith is placed in unintended consequences because of the belief that "welfare related, foreign and defense issues are primary."[12] Although there are differences in emphasis among the neofunctionalists, including Haas, on economic redistribution and Lindberg and Scheingold's stress on political interaction, they fundamentally hold to the concepts of incremental impact, spillover, and other components of this general framework.

Although Haas restricts himself to these three classifications, there are trends indicating that two other approaches will become more widely used. These approaches include systems analysis, which has basic roots in neofunctionalism, and what is referred to here as the "combination" school. It should be noted at this point that each school is deficient in both theory and research strategy. Rarely do integration analyses provide adequate causal explanation. These approaches will soon be discussed in detail; however, the marked difference between approaches is primarily in the area of research strategies and methods. Research approaches thus reflect different concepts of integration.

The systems approach is an offshoot of general international systems theory applied on a regional basis. Although David Easton may be considered to be the initiator,[13] there are far more sophisticated frameworks being applied to the international arena. Indeed, some of these approaches can only be traced to Easton as an initiator of the basic conceptual framework, with little resemblance to that model in their present form. These include those of Michael Brecher,[14] Stanley Hoffman,[15] Morton Kaplan,[16] and Richard Rosecrance.[17] Emphasis has been on what constitutes a system within a geographic area and how this system interacts with the international system. Issue areas are examined with a view, to use Kaplan's terminology, to what is "sub-system dominant"[18] (the predominant issue area). "Sub-system dominance" may be within the context of what Brecher would term, for example, a "subordinate system" or regional system, such as the Middle East.[19] Although systems analysis is state-centric, there is frequently analysis of issue areas that are not directly the product of direct political authority, that is, through governments. In systems terms, governments are the traditional source of what Easton terms the "authoritative allocation of values."[20] Non-state-centric approaches would look to other sources, such as interest groups, for authority sources or integrating forces.

The "combination" school seeks to utilize what its advocates believe to be the best of the neofunctionalist and communications schools. There is criticism of both approaches. Most frequently the shortcomings of the communications school are cited, so this type of analysis is at best seen as an empirical base for neofunctionalism, meaning transactional data are used. A neofunctionalist believes in "spillover," whereby collective decisions made on one issue will affect others incrementally. The result is an unintended impact on related but unforeseen issues within the regional area. A regional decision, for example, about import policy may affect labor relations, which, in turn, may affect company law. The consequence of all this is movement toward supranationality or political integration. The combination theorists seek rigor in empirical analysis and often look to the type of transaction analysis found in communications theory as an appropriate methodology. This is because communications theory offers what is viewed by "combinationists" as the great deficiency of neofunctionalism—a rigorous tool for research in the form of aggregate data collection. Frequently they seek "linkage" between the two approaches.

Haas, a neofunctionalist who uses some communications concepts, has developed a "master concept" of linkage. This is "authority-legitimacy transfer" whereby certain economic and social indicators are "earlier points" for political integration.[21] To some extent, Haas also has systems-oriented goals. He indicates a desire for "an effectiveness model in which the criterion of success is the transformation of the international system to a higher level of integration as opposed to maintenance."[22] This is a reduction to a smaller scale of the Rosecrance model whereby transformation indicators were key elements for establishing criteria of different stages of the international system.

### Major Differences Between Conceptual Frameworks and Resulting Research Strategies

Integration theory, as has been seen, is concerned with the dynamics of "noncoercive" interaction[23] between political units, usually the state, that result in regional association. The neofunctionalist asks, what is the impact of a decision and what is the motivation of the actor? The actor is usually viewed as a self-interested institution or national leader within what Haas calls the "modern pluralistic-industrial democratic polity."[24] The end product in neofunctionalism does not have a precise definition. However, institutional regionalism, for example, the EEC, is an indication of what the neofunctionalist sees as an integration unit.

Communications theory poses the question, what is the rate of transaction between states? Transaction flows, to a communications theorist, indicate the absence or presence of a regional unit, that is, a community. Even the concept of boundaries is not a result of institutionalized decision making, but "a place where there is a critical reduction in the frequency of a certain type of transaction."[25] Integration is defined by Deutsch as "a relationship among units in which they are mutually interdependent and jointly produce system properties which they separately lack."[26] The end result of integration in the communications framework is a "pluralistic security community." The preconditions for this are a degree of value compatibility, predictability of behavior, and unbroken links of social communication.[27]

### Integrationist Approaches to Research

The differing questions and ends posed by both integrationist schools have led to different approaches to research. Some of these differences will be demonstrated by reviewing the work of Donald Puchala, Haas, and B. Hughes and J. Schwarz. How each of these authors views the role of mass communities is indicative of the different conceptual framework and research strategy of each school.

Each school examines different kinds of data to analyze the integration process. The neofunctionalist will review the output of institutions as well as of nation-states to determine levels of integration. There is more concern with the style of decision making, shared values, and compliance with decisions, and there is stress upon major economic redistributive and peace/war issues. The communications theorist reviews aggregate data to determine rate of transaction, regardless of the issue, and gives equal weight to all variables. He views his research strategy as more empirically rigorous than neofunctionalism. Neofunctionalist research will place more stress upon the role of the actor. This is frequently accomplished through organizational case studies, such as Haas's work on the ILO in *Beyond the Nation-State.* The communications theorist will be further removed from the actor because he is looking only at outputs that can be measured.

Donald Puchala, a student of Deutsch, explores various measures of regional integration within the communications school.[28] He is concerned with the impact of communications links upon sovereignty. Although he finds various measures to be satisfactory for their particular intended purpose, he sees integration analysis today as "moving from functional sector to functional sector."[29] Theory should show "whys and hows of periodic incremental reductions in national sovereignty and conditional expansion in supranational activity."[30] It should also indicate the development of consensus integration at both "elite and mass levels."[31]

Puchala firmly believes in the Deutschian concept of political amalgamation whereby states become politically integrated into a supranational body. Transaction flows are viewed as an appropriate means of measuring this progress. However, the neofunctionalist concept of spillover trends "channeled into political institutions"[32] must be measured. Transaction analysis, over time, is a good means for doing this.[33] Puchala emphasizes that transactional interaction between nongovernment groups and their relationship to regional "rulemaking institutions" must be tracked.[34] On a note of caution he adds, "As yet, however, it is not completely clear to me exactly how the mass populations enter into the international social assimilation process."[35]

Deutsch himself has a partial answer to Puchala's query when he delineates three stages of an integration: leadership by intellectuals, great politicians assume a major role, and mass movements and/or large-scale elite politics.[36] Deutsch believes that most integrationist movements do not move through these states concurrently, but in steps.[37] Thus, elite politics/mass movements plan a reactive role to signals from what Deutsch calls a "core area."[38] The core is "one or more of a few political units which are stronger and more highly developed than the remaining constituent parts." It is through this process that "partial integration occurs because minor specific transnational tasks are delegated to a regional agency or supranational body."[39] Integration is a function of the strength and development of a core area and not a development of incremental effects or spillover from decision making as the neofunctionalist would posit in Deutsch's framework.

Thus, Deutsch's concept of integration is not state-centric, although transaction analysis has been used primarily as a measure of national/transnational political integration. Inherently there appears to be greater flexibility for a non-state-centric approach by using communications theory rather than neofunctionalism. The actor is virtually synonymous with nation in the neofunctionalist literature, although case studies of organizations test a broader concept of supranationality.

The neofunctionalist view of process is highlighted through the writing of P. C. Schmitter. Schmitter argues that there may be "no cumulative trend at all" when the process of political integration is "plotted over time."[40] However, he firmly believes that the most direct route is "by way of successive spillovers or package deals involving new issues and new competences."[41] The external environment may give rise to "unexpected performance."[42] Thus, Schmitter sees the external environment affecting the unintentionality of spillover. However, more sophisticated, quasi-planned package deals make the process more deliberate than originally postulated by Haas. This is Schmitter's "revision," but, will be seen, when compared to Nye, in a conceptual sense, he does not deviate as far from the original neofunctionalist model. Perhaps this can be attributed to Schmitter's greater concern (than Nye's) with methodology.

The neofunctionalists have responded to Puchala's query concerning the role of mass populations by minimizing their role. Hughes and Schwarz[43] indicate that Lindberg and Scheingold, two leading exponents of the neofunctionalist school, see mass communities as "a background variable which conditioned but did not determine growth processes in the community" (EEC).[44] However, they believe that a relationship exists "between intergovernmental cooperation at the diplomatic level, the institutional growth of the EEC [similar to Deutsch's concept of political amalgamation] and the unity of the European populations [mass community]."[45] They note that changes in intergovernment cooperation preceded major instances of community institutional change and these preceded "good feelings among the community population."[46]

The place of mass activity as noted is deemphasized in both the communications and functionalist schools, although the communications school places more emphasis on this research through transaction analysis. Communications theory sees links between peoples as very important, regardless of national boundaries. Measurable cooperation across national borders is a significant test of community and it is conceivable that research could indicate greater communication ties between than within national borders. Hughes and Schwarz believe that mass communities should be an added component to the definition of an integrationist end. They presently see two contexts being referred to by both communications theorists and neofunctionists: "political amalgamation" or "the use of central organizations which link states together" and intergovernment cooperation in the diplomatic arena other than through a central organization. The latter concept is similar to Deutsch's "pluralistic security community."[47]

Hughes and Schwarz, in the tradition of combination theorists, propose that in addition to these two a third end be added, that of "mass community" or the extent to which "attitudes of friendship and closeness appear among the populations of these states."[48] Of course, this brings us back to the traditional problem of integration theory—is integration a means or an end? Does it refer to process or an ideal state? There is no clear-cut answer in the current literature.

L. J. Cantori and S. L. Spiegel note that the future of the dependent variable problem must be resolved by determining whether integration is viewed as a process or a terminal state. This is particularly a conceptual problem for the neofunctionalists, as political integration is "an ideal to be sought."[49] Cantori and Spiegel identify two other conceptual problems that are particular to the neofunctionalists:

1. The "apolitical character of their analysis." The concern with economic variables and incremental decisions leading to almost "inadvertent" political integration is distressing to them.[50] They do note that Schmitter, a leading neofunctionalist, states that "relevant actors" have strategies that are "eminently political."[51]
2. There is a lack of concern with "external powers" and their effect on regional integration.[52]

They conclude that the integrative (or combination) approach is inappropriate as a "vestige of the level of analysis problem and the lack of specification about the dependent variable" (political integration).[53]

Etzioni agrees with Cantori and Spiegel's point about the definition of integration. He clearly sees political integration as a terminal state.[54] Etzioni traces his "epigenesis" framework to Detusch and Talcott Parsons. The "epigenesis model suggests some social units acquire new subunits that fulfill new functions rather than just provide new subunits for functions served before in a less specialized manner."[55] Etzioni is concerned with the locus and distribution of power between and within integrated units.

Boundaries to Etzioni are a key concept in determining power relations. Apparently this is an amplification of Deutsch's core nation in view of Etzioni's acknowledgment of Deutsch's influence.[56] Etzioni is also concerned with decision making as process. Indeed, he indicates that the "take off" of supranational authority is dependent upon the amount of international decision making required.[57] Therefore, integration is not a "linear" process, but subject to the neofunctionalist concept of spillover.

Etzioni is not primarily involved with methodological issues. He clearly states his position, places himself primarily in the communications camp methodologically, and acknowledges the functionalist influence of Parsons. He attempts to correct the deficiencies of neofunctionalism by developing the epigenesis model, which primarily concerns the development of spillover. This may be a fruitful direction, but because methodological problems have not been solved, it would be interesting to see how Etzioni applies his model to a particular region.

Etzioni offers a precise definition of integration, something not frequently done by theorists of both communications and neofunctionalism. It is noteworthy that he has attempted to build a model that addresses this deficiency in integration theory.

To summarize, communications and neofunctionalist approaches to integration theory do not rigorously define political integration. There is confusion about whether it is a process or an end. Furthermore, the two leading approaches of analysis, communications and neofunctionalism, appear to be heading toward a synthesis, both conceptually and methodologically. The role of mass populations in the integration process has not been satisfactorily answered by either approach.

Given the previously mentioned deficiency of communications and neofunctionalist analysis, the need for an eclectic approach to empirical research becomes apparent. This is accomplished by what is termed the combination theorists, and it is to them that we must turn for the most assistance in analyzing the impact of regional integration upon a transnational issue area.

## The Combination Approach

C. Bergsten, Robert Keohane, and Nye address Cantori and Spiegel's point concerning the "apolitical character" of neofunctionalist analysis. Bergsten, Keohane, and Nye indicate that there is a close connection between political and economic "factors" on the "motivational level." This connection is so close that they are intertwined.[58] They argue that economic or "welfare" goals have replaced the use of violence, which they imply is the basis (unrealized potential) of political action. Since welfare goals are now of primary importance, two new actors must be considered as major: "a number of countries previously considered unimportant and transnational economic actors of which multinational enterprises are the most important."[59]

Nye expands his position by relating it to neofunctionalism.[60] Nye believes that neofunctional analysis is more appropriate where a strong institutional framework already exists as opposed to "loosely structured relationships."[61] He notes the importance of technocrats and interest groups that pressure government to create a regional economic organization. Once this is accomplished, a flow of transaction is unleashed with potential for a political unit.[62] Although he does not state it, one would think that in view of this, Nye would view transaction/communications analysis as a means of testing the cohesiveness of an already existing institutional structure.

Nye is one of the few analysts of neofunctionalism who views the external environment as an important force for integration. Indeed, he notes it as a pressure point upon mass opinion for regional economic association.[63] This highlights the importance of Cantori and Spiegel's point about the importance of external powers and links it to Puchala's concern about mass communities. Nye as a theorist of regional integration almost stands by himself. In a sense he is the bridgehead to systems analysis. He is concerned not only with the appropriate use of standard neofunctional and transaction analysis but also with the psychological dimension and the place of interest groups in the integrative process.

## Private Interest Groups as a Transnational Actor

Nye notes that regional integration stimulates private groups "to create various types of formal and informal non-governmental regional organizations."[64] In his opinion, they generally remain a weak force, that is:

> Despite the existence of regional trade union secretariats in Brussels, the idea of collective bargaining at the European level in response to

the creation of a European market has not taken hold—in part because of the division in the labor movement but also because of the importance of national government power in collective bargaining ... the most important source of power for interest groups still remains at the national level.[65]

The question of the role of trade union secretariats will be discussed more fully in subsequent chapters. At this point it should be noted that Nye believes private interest groups are extremely important to the integration process, whether in terms of the formation of formal national political integration or other integrative groupings that exercise power across national boundaries. This occurs through what Nye terms "cultivated spillover" or "package deals." In this process elite groups bargain and form conditions and linkages across national boundaries, frequently knowing the consequences of their actions. This is a refined view of Haas's incremental concept of spillover. Nye believes that the greater the pluralism of modern associational groups (that is, labor unions), the better the condition for an integrative response.[66]

Lindberg and Scheingold also review the impact of interest groups, particularly in Europe.[67] They, like Nye, view the primary role of interest groups as a cohesive function once an institutional context has been developed: "Faced with the emergence of a new decision-making system, groups have organized across national boundaries so as to maintain contacts, secure information and seek access to policy makers."[68] They indicate that interest groups have formed at the community level, and this they see as an "adaptation" on the part of economic elites.[69]

Lindberg and Scheingold have identified a methodology for defining the cohesiveness of integration at the institutional level. Although they intend to use this as an indicator of "intensity" of integration, it is quite possible to apply this to the integration process prior to the formation of a formal institutional structure. They identify 22 functions, including labor-management relations and determine where the locus of decision making is for each. They plot this on a scale of 1 to 5 (high to low integration). This then allows Lindberg and Scheingold to see to what extent decisions are made at the regional level with "that of the nation-state acting more or less unilaterally."[70] The data are then viewed over time and ranked by level of decision making, indicating what problems "confront the community as a whole and require some kind of joint response ... also the gathering of information and the development of alternative solutions."[71] Thus predecisional inputs are a necessity for examining the level of intensity for integration. In all probability, Deutsch would agree with this form of neofunctionalism, although his methodology would assign equal weight to all factors. Lindberg and Scheingold therefore view integration more as a process than as an end. Lindberg stated in 1963 that political integration was the "process whereby nations forego the desire to conduct foreign and key domestic policy independently."[72] His later writings confirm this view.

Combination theorists rely primarily on the communications and neofunctionalist schools, disregarding systems analysis. This is the approach used here—transactional analysis coupled with neofunctionalist/integrationalist concepts.

## Systems Analysis

The systems analyst offers a new perspective owing much to the pioneering framework of Easton.[73] The literature in this area is far-reaching and voluminous; however, as applied to regional integration, it is only beginning to come into its own. A landmark work in this area is *The Foreign Policy System of Israel* by Brecher.[74] It is a direct application of "A Framework for Research on Foreign Policy Behavior."[75] Although the primary concern is with foreign policy outputs, it treats a geographic area, the Middle East, as a separate and distinct "system." Brecher postulates six present "subordinate" systems that are characterized by

1) Delimited scope with primary stress on a geographic region;
2) At least three actors;
3) Objective recognition by most other actors as constituting a distinctive community, region or segment of the global system;
4) Self-identification as such;
5) Units of power relatively inferior to units in the dominant system, using a sliding scale of power in both; and,
6) Greater effect on the subordinate system by penetration from the dominant system than the reverse.[76]

Brecher thus has rigorously defined an integrated unit or "subordinate system" that he then relates to behavior and structure within the international system. He stipulates a number of variables for analysis of a system—and indeed a state—including the role of interest groups. Brecher uses Gabriel Almond's classification[77] of interest groups and states that they perform two functions: "In a foreign policy system: they communicate information about the environment to the decision-making elite and they may also advocate policies to those who wield authority in the system."[78] Thus, interest groups have an influential and definitional function within a subordinate system.

Interest groups may exercise their function in the systems framework along similar parameters to those described by the neofunctionalists. The concern is not with formal organizational units, but with interaction among core states. Frequently there is an institutional structure linking the core with what Brecher terms the "periphery." Communication is an important element, but by no means is it as important in systems analysis as it is in the Deutschian framework. Indeed it is only one "textural feature" among others.[79]

Systems analysis allows a rigorous descriptive framework for viewing the level of political integration as well as foreign policy outputs. To date, it has not been as empirically effective for comparing levels of integration or determining intensity. However, there has been success in determining outputs of integrated systems as well as providing a useful framework for historical analysis.

To date, all approaches to regional integration have been primarily concerned with the political unification of nations. Etzioni sees this as an end, the neofunctionalists generally posit this as an ideal, and the communications analysts emphasize the preintegrative period. Systems analysts posit geographic configurations to determine foreign policy outputs with a view to determining the nature of the international state system. Although all three approaches are concerned with interest groups or mass populations, few analysts examine input outside the state structure or consider forms of supranationality other than formal politically integrative institutions.

## Can Integration Theory Be Applied to Non-State-Centric Research?

So far, the discussion has focused primarily upon the role of the state as actor. It has been noted that Nye has worked in the area of private interest groups as transnational actors, and that transaction analysis, a methodological tool of the communications school, offers great potential for non-state-centric research. The works of Brecher, Haas, and Helen Feldstein are indicative of how integration theory in its present form can be applied to non-state-centric research, either at the level of interest groups or individual as sector.

Brecher, who is closer to the systems school of international relations, is concerned with the psychological dimension, particularly actor perception. He notes two external environments, the operational and the psychological.[80] Frequently, these environments coincide. Brecher indicates case examples of actor perception effect on regional integration.[81] Nye is also centrally concerned about the role of actor perception.[82] In his discussion concerning the role of the external environment, he indicates that an "integrative condition" is the perception of the regional actor of potential equity in a union.[83] Nye does not go as far in the development of a theory of psychological environment; however, he does think that the "complementarity" of elite values as a psychological input is important. The degree to which elite groups hold similar values is indicative of the potential for integrative success.[84] If elite groups are able to negotiate and reduce their initial "visible" costs, potential integration is closer to reality.[85]

Without further exploration of the psychological dimension, it should be noted that this framework is relevant to integrationist theory and offers a fruitful area for further research.

Two studies that do attempt less of a non-state-centric approach are Haas's neofunctionalist study of the ILO[86] and Feldstein's communications analysis.[87] As both of these studies are concerned with labor, it would appear that labor research has significant implications for integration analysis.

Haas's framework has already been discussed. His case study of the ILO is an attempt to explore how supranational this body has become, primarily by examining its success within its own terms over time. Haas notes that the ILO's objectives have changed at various periods because of fear of impingement of sovereignty on member states. Thus, by settling for a goal of instituting minimal labor standards, the ILO has achieved what Nye would call the "least visible cost." Haas summarizes actual compliance with ILO recommended standards and concludes that this UN body has not been very successful as a supranational organization. He briefly mentions the international trade secretariats, but dismisses their role in the integration process because of lack of success at international collective bargaining.[88]

In 1960, this may have been true; however, Haas was shortsighted to limit his conclusions about the role of ITSs to international collective bargaining. Other forms of cooperation, including those requiring a high level of trade union power, such as international sympathy strikes, could have been analyzed within the ITS context. By restricting himself to the only worldwide labor body in which governments participate, the ILO, Haas overlooked other potentially integrative institutions. This is perhaps an indication of the myopia of a government-oriented institutional framework. Haas did not explore the potential supranationality of mass communities (labor) through their interest groups (national/international labor unions).

Feldstein's work is of particular interest because she has studied transnational labor activity within the EEC utilizing the communications school. Feldstein acknowledges that she is heavily influenced by Deutsch.[89] She focuses "on movement of workers across national boundaries within the EEC."[90] Her study is a good example of the application of transaction analysis across national boundaries.

Feldstein expands Haas's concept of the process of political integration whereby actors "shift their loyalties, expectations and political activities toward a new center, whose institutions possess or demand jurisdiction over the preexisting national states."[91] She states that integration must be defined to include "the individual workers involved in the transaction process."[92]

Feldstein studied transaction data across national boundaries within the original six of the EEC and the United Kingdom. Her data concerns the migration of workers within this area, and she attempts to make some conclusions about the interaction level of migrating groups to foreign countries. From this she makes some tentative statements about worker perception of community, but she realizes that there is need for further study of the psychological ties that are or are not created as a result of labor migration. She concludes that

> at the level of the Six, it has become increasingly apparent that the cultural, social, economic and technical difficulties inherent in this form of transaction are being met within the Community cadre by improvement in coordination and cooperation.[93]
>
> In a transaction form which involves the flow of individuals across national borders, it is precisely through this sort of connection that meaningful communication, transaction and the ongoing process of integration may become mutually reinforcing.[94]

Feldstein thus expands Haas's concept of integration to include the development of community ties established by the transaction or interchange of individuals—workers. She utilizes Deutsch's method of transaction analysis to determine the degree of interaction and makes tentative statements about the implications for political integration. Feldstein's approach indicates the relevance of studying labor transactions across national boundaries. It is of and by itself related to the process of political integration whether or not a supranational authority such as the ILO exists. Furthermore, there are implications for political integration, according to Feldstein, even if there is no direct state input.[95]

Thus, Haas and Feldstein share a view that transnational labor research can serve as a meaningful indication of political integration. Although Haas is a neofunctionalist concerned with supranational institutions and Feldstein is a communications theorist emphasizing international worker transactions, they both believe that increased ties between labor organizations and/or workers forges an increased community of interest. This is an essential component of political integration in both frameworks.

## The Relevant Framework

The liberal-functionalist approach within the multinational literature, coupled with communications integration theory, offers a fruitful conceptual design for conducting transnational labor research. The liberal-functionalist sees the MNC as a new and positive force. Although MNCs have roots in the industrial revolution as Marx well recognized, the communications, data collection, and global management strategy of the modern MNC are of a new order. The question of whether the labor movement also sees MNCs as a positive force is a normative concern that can best be answered by looking at the data in subsequent chapters. However, the liberal-functionalist approach appears to be closest to the reality of the present-day MNC; and because the integrative capacity of the MNC is stressed in this framework, it would appear to be the most useful.

The communications school offers an excellent means for organizing and interpreting quantifiable data. Questionnaire responses will indicate transnational transactions and thus be a measure of communications as defined by this school of integration theory.

The literature on MNCs and political integration are not a relevant conceptual framework by themselves. This study thus will selectively use each to develop what is hopefully a synergistic combination for a transnational labor relations research framework. This will, therefore, not be a purist approach. A straightforward reliance on transaction data as a strict communicationist would have it will not occur; nor will there be a disregard of rigorous data collection, as is a hallmark of the neofunctionalist school.

As previously indicated, there is a paucity of data on transnational labor activity. Therefore, this study will take steps toward closing this gap and be concerned with the movement, coordination, and cooperation of workers within Europe (to a lesser extent elsewhere) across national borders. Focus will be upon their relationship to MNCs, which Nye notes (and most major authors would be in agreement) have a "global management strategy." Furthermore, Nye states: "The important point is that direct investment creates a transnational interdependence which groups or governments try to manipulate for their own political purpose."[96] It would seem useful for the social scientists to ask: How have labor movements reacted to this transnational interdependence, and what are the implications for political integration?

The relationship between workers and those who control capital has, of course, been a central question in political science. However, this has always been placed in the context of the nation-state. The advent of the MNC adds a new dimension, because to some extent MNCs have become a more significant integrative force and authority source to organized labor than the nation-state.

Although the total impact of the MNC on integration is beyond the scope of this work, the worker organization response within an economically integrated area (the Common Market)—particularly in those areas where there is a centralization of multinationals—will be tested. The impact of this study, other than the empirical data presented for integration analysis, hopefully will be a contribution to a neglected area of political science: transnational interest group analysis.

The success of the analysis of a specific interest group—labor unions—across national boundaries should indicate the empirical utility of this approach for further integration studies. The application may be relevant for what Almond and J. Coleman term "non-associational interest groups" as well as organized groups.[97]

Integration analysis, when placed in a context of a newly emerging power, the multinational, may be fruitful for interest group theory as well as a non-state-centric paradigm for political science. This study will view integration as a process, not a terminal state. Operationally that process will be tested by Haas's definition of that process—noncoercive interaction between political units.[98] The focus will be on trade unions, the primary organizational unit for the representation of those in the work place.

Concepts from communications theory will also be utilized. Transnational flows across national borders will be tracked to determine union cooperation among themselves and between them and the MNCs. Furthermore, tentative statements will be made about political integration.

## THE MULTINATIONAL LITERATURE

The literature on the multinational corporation with respect to their impact on labor can be broken down into three perspectives: (1) the Marxist view, which posits economic imperialism resulting in exploitation of the worker; (2) the liberal-functionalist view, which commonly sees multinationals as a positive force for world peace and stability with a generally beneficial impact on workers' standard of living; and (3) the minor impact view, which sees multinationals as not having a significant effect on labor. Additionally, there are observers who do not fully subscribe to the minor impact view but believe it is too soon for a conclusion to be reached about the impact of MNCs on labor.

## The Marxist View

Economics as an integrating force is a recurrent theme throughout political science. Marx, writing in the *Manifesto* as early as 1848, saw manufacturing as being a function of the "giant, modern industry" controlling a "world market."[99] The bourgeoisie was the product of a series of political advances that had at its root economic exploitation. The highest state of bourgeoisie development was reached when "old-established national industries have been destroyed" to be replaced by industries capable of extracting raw materials from "the remotest zones; industries whose products are consumed, not only at home, but in every quarter of the globe."[100] What are the workers left with in their struggle with the bourgeoisie? Marx noted that as a result of the process of capitalist development, workers form "combinations"—or trade unions—which, because of the "improved means of communications which are created by modern industry, and which place the workers of different localities in contact with one another,"[101] strengthen the union of labor.

The concept of the multinational corporation engendering a need for trade unions to cooperate is thus not a new idea. At least 100 years before the sophisticated concept of transfer pricing, Marx spoke of the development of "multinational" industry and the concurrent growth of ties developing between labor unions between countries or, in modern terminology, "transnationally." To Marx this was a matter of historical development based upon class struggle. This economic development has at its very roots transnational centralization of labor struggle against giant industry.

V. I. Lenin expanded upon multinational "finance capital" as an integrating force. To Lenin imperialism was "the highest stage of capitalism" and its development was reached by "the intense struggle waged against other nation/state groups of financiers for the division of the world and domination over other countries.[102] The abolition of free competition under monopoly capitalism was the work of giant cartels—internationally. Indeed, the carving up of the world's electricity and oil markets by financial trusts is what Lenin specifically finds as the function of capitalist imperialism exploitation.

Lenin saw his pamphlet on imperialism as a "manifesto" in, of course, the same tradition as Marx.[103] Although much of it is an attack on Karl Kautsky, the primary purpose is to awaken the proletariat to the then current stages of capitalist development. Lenin was showing empirically why it was necessary for labor to develop transnational ties to combat the exploitation of the international cartel.

The Marxist critique of multinational industry and its thesis that economics is an integrating force is supported by the contemporary writer André Gorz. Gorz writes of what he perceives to be the coming class struggle in Europe as a result of economic integration plans prompted by the development of the EEC. He presents a specific strategy for labor based upon the assumption that "the tendency toward the internationalization of production is an objective process linked to the dimensions, the degree of specialization and the cost of a productive apparatus which incorporates modern technology."[104] Gorz's strategy is an attempt to some extent for labor to fight the integration of the world economy. Part of his argument is that the "developed capitalist societies, for better or for worse, integrate the struggles of the working classes."[105]

Marx, Lenin, and Gorz each saw the expansion of the industrial base across national frontiers as the inevitable product of capitalist development. The impact on labor would be to form "combinations" to engage in a collective struggle. Because these "combinations" would have a transnational interest as a result of worldwide cartelization and subsequent exploitation, it could be expected that unions would develop an international strategy. This is rooted in the historical process of economic development.

## The Liberal-Functionalist View

The liberal-functionalist proposition is that multinationals are a "new institution for world economic and social integration, prefiguring a global society. It is apt to maximize welfare internationally if its role is understood by the nation-state and labor which have to acquire a world-wide outlook."[106]

Hans Gunter and Howard Perlmutter have attempted to present a theoretical framework for the liberal-functionalist approach encompassing both the trade union and the multinational. However, most studies having this perspective are concerned with empirical issues in labor relations. Thus there are works by David Blake,[107] Duane Kujawa,[108] and John Crispo,[109] which are primarily concerned with the auto industry in North America, frequently under the guise of "international trade unionism." The concept of linking the impact of U.S. (and European) multinational corporations to the multinational trade union movement outside of North America has been little more than an appendix to the general multinational corporation literature. Blake,[110] Perlmutter,[111] Gunter,[112] Charles Levinson,[113] and certain trade union specialists, primarily at U.K. universities[114] and the Paris-based Organization for Economic Cooperation and Development (OEDC)[115] have recently contributed to this area of trade union literature.

Gunter has theoretical concerns about the future of transnational industrial relations and he relies heavily upon Perlmutter's classification of multinationals. The classification is concerned with the locus of decision making in a multinational. If decisions are home-country based, they are "ethnocentric" multinationals. A greater dispersion of decision-making authorities leads to "geocentric" management. Perlmutter makes other more subtle distinctions in his descriptions of criteria for these categories. However, the primary criterion is the locus of decision making.[116] Gunter uses the Perlmutter classification to "tentatively explain the propensity of industrial relations to transnationalize."[117] The variables Gunter sees as "relevant" are the multinational management approach to labor relations and the "transnational power of unions."[118] Thus Gunter is concerned with power and style.

Perlmutter believes that "at the heart of the matter is the vulnerability of the geocentric multinational firm that seeks economies between subsidiaries."[119] Thus, the multinational in the Perlmutter and Gunter context represents a structural change in the world's economy, which, by virtue of its global management capacity, ultimately presents a significant challenge to trade unions.

Gunter has developed a useful "box model" incorporating the Perlmutter classification (see Figure 1.1). The objective of the model is to crystallize various stages of transnational industrial relations and to offer a level of prediction about what will occur transnationally at each stage of multinational development. Thus in square 1 in Figure 1.1, the locus for decision making for both unions and management remains at the national level. In squares 3 and 4 a development to "bilateral transnational industrial relations" will occur, leading ultimately to "international collective bargaining."[120]

Gunter notes that the box model must be coupled with a review of environmental factors that are regionally specific, that is, the political and economic system.[121] He does not relate the environmental factors with stages of multinational development. In Gunter's model the lack of causality between the variables delineated is a major weakness for allowing prediction or gaining heuristic insight into transnational labor trends. However, the model is an excellent framework for categorization of stages of transnational development.

The Gunter framework should be compared with that of H. Perlmutter, as it is Perlmutter who presents the structure for Gunter. Perlmutter is an exponent of a "geocentrizing" world economy. He holds with the school of thought that maintains multinationals will create a better social order by promoting peace, stability, and economic wellbeing. He does not offer a specific model other than his previously referred to classification system. Perlmutter's concern with respect to trade unions is their role in the geocentrizing process—particularly,

**FIGURE 1.1**  Gunter's Box Model

Propensity of Industrial Relations to Transnationalize

|  |  | Transnational Power of Unions[a] | | | |
|---|---|---|---|---|---|
|  |  | Small | | Great | |
| Behavioral Pattern of Multinational Corporations[b] | Polycentric | Unilateral Low | Bilateral Low | Unilateral Low | Bilateral Low |
|  |  | (1) | | (2) | |
|  | Ethno- and Geocentric | Unilateral High | Bilateral Low | Unilateral Low | Bilateral High |
|  |  | (3) | | (4) | |

[a] Exerted, for example, through coordinated national strategies or the threat to use such strategies.

[b] Regarding decisions of prime interest to labor (work rules and economic issues affecting employment).

how do they interact with the state and the multinational in this process?

It is Perlmutter's contention that multinational firms are "geocentrizing" at a faster rate than either unions or states.[122] The multinational is becoming the worldwide institution of dominance and that "neither host nor home nation states are overwhelming countervailing forces because essentially individual states compete for the resources and capabilities of multinational firms ... it is probably to the interest of the trade union to seek to share in the wealth produced by the multinational firm."[123]

Perlmutter's research design is a two-way classification. He builds a matrix of organization types (state, multinational firm, or trade union) and obstacles to their development (geo-, ethno-, polycentric) and then examines each in detail. Environmental forces working on each of these three institutions are examined as well as "intra" or forces that, because of the nature of the institutions, will affect the extent of globalization. Thus, with respect to trade unions, Perlmutter sees the "economic integration in Europe and Latin America" (environmental force) and "emerging leadership committed to an international organization approach to organization" (internal force) as positive trends toward "geocentrism." Variations in size of domestic markets (environmental force) and "limited international managerial resources of world-wide unions" (internal force) are negative forces.[124]

Perlmutter's classification scheme is used as an organizing framework for speculation about potential globalization. He does not present data within this content, although the table of environmental and "intra" factors could be used for this. Indeed, Perlmutter indicates that there is a need for further research in this area, particularly with respect to his projections about the rapid rate of multinational geocentrizing and the "process by which nations, unions, and multinational firms collaborate to reach common objectives."[125]

Thus both Perlmutter and Gunter believe that the "geocentrizing," or in Barnet and Muller's term "globalization," process is essentially one of collaboration between institutions. Perlmutter maintains that under certain circumstances coalitions may develop between unions and the state against multinationals or some combination thereof will occur. The research in this volume will indicate the development of union strategy as a "geocentrizing" institution vis-a-vis the multinational corporation; however, coalition building will not be addressed. The primary reason for this is that national legislatures have not been viewed as an arena for coalition building for other interest groups to obtain legislation against MNCs. They see transnational rather than national action as more fruitful.

Perlmutter and Gunter agree that the basic impact of the multinational is salutary. Although Gunter qualifies this by saying that in developed areas there is little difference between wages and benefits paid by multinationals when compared to locally owned firms, the contrary is true in developing nations.[126] Gunter does agree with Perlmutter's basic hypothesis that unions have lagged in the transnationalization process when compared to the multinational corporation.[127] Although Gunter tends to be more critical of the multinational corporation and recognizes the merit of other views of the multinational— particularly that the multinational is an economic imperialist—he and Perlmutter essentially subscribe to the liberal view that multinationals primarily have had a beneficial impact on labor and that trade unions have not been able to keep up with their transnational pace.

### The Minor Impact View

The proposition that MNCs essentially are not a new phenomenon (Marx would have agreed) and have not had a significant impact on transnational labor relations is a recurrent theme of H. Northrup, R. Rowan, and W. Curtin. They believe that the MNC impact is overrated and publicity is out of proportion to what in reality has occurred.

Northrup and Rowan have attempted to confirm the claims of Levinson about the "major role" the International Chemical Workers Federation has had in coordinating labor activities at Akzo, Monsanto, Solvay, Michelin, and other companies. In each instance he reports that Levinson's claims are not accurate and that he has capitalized on the efforts of other unions. Northrup and Rowan interviewed the management of each of these companies; and, at Michelin and Akzo, the management denied meeting with Levinson—contrary to his claims.[128] Northrup and Rowan are therefore saying that Levinson and the ICF's claims are overblown. They do believe that other forms of coordinated transnational labor activity have occurred, particularly through the European Metal Workers Federation.[129] However, if the claims of the ICF are discounted, much of what is publicly reported as transnational labor activity can be disregarded. Levinson is presently planning a refutation of the Northrup and Rowan article. Their essential point is that there has been less transnational labor activity than documented as a result of multinational growth. The data I have gathered, although not specifically directed to the ICF transactions, does not specifically deny or confirm their view. However, in a statistical sense, based upon union claims and even discounting them to a certain extent, it does appear that there is more to this as a trend than Northrup and Rowan indicate, especially with respect to the ICF.

Curtin, after reviewing the obstacles to international collective bargaining, particularly those of a legal nature, and the structure of the international trade union movement has inserted a normative view about the future of transnational labor relations: "Meaningful collective bargaining at the multinational level appears to be neither feasible nor particularly desirable."[130]

The pro-management orientation of Curtin (and of Northrup and Rowan) is reflected in his desire to prevent multinational collective bargaining from developing. Levinson may have overstated his case; however, apparently management-oriented analysts are minimizing what has occurred. Curtin has examined both the structural nature of international labor relations and international labor law and rightly concludes that the obstacles for transnational labor are numerous. However, he has not looked at what has actually occurred—as will be done in the following chapters.

Another management-oriented analyst, David Barran of Shell Oil, has a similar view to W. Curtin's, that of minimizing the role of the multinational on transnational labor relations. In a refutation of the British Trades Union Congress (the trades union federation in the United Kingdom representing almost all unions) position,[131] Barran indicates that unions have a lack of understanding about how MNCs operate. "In practice," Barran states, "the multilateral enterprise is simply the latest phase in the development of commercial mechanisms to handle the international movement of goods and services ... but that does not mean that MNC's are able to ride rough-shod over the laws and practices of the countries in which the constituent enterprises do business."[132] He argues that as a function of decentralization of management, industrial relations policies are a function of local management and the company is more interested in individual participation than trade unionism.

Barran's statement may be considered as typical of the management view. The decentralization of policy indicates that each location within the corporation conducts its own policies; thus national labor relations have little input from the worldwide body. Indeed, each country's profits must be treated separately in negotiations for the purpose of adjusting wages and benefits. Thus workers have no transnational interests. The MNC has not structurally changed anything except to create more locally based enterprises. When international trade union strategy is examined, the union perspective of the management argument will be examined. However, at this time it should be noted that management, as represented by Barran and Curtin (as well as some questionnaires discussed in Chapter 4), tends to adhere to the minor impact view. By so doing, management essentially rejects what Barnet and Muller term the "international division of labor," which these authors say is at the core of their strategy.[133] From this strategic base, management can personally argue that only national interests should prevail for workers and that local practice must be followed.

It is this author's view that as unions become more aggressive against the MNC, the minor impact view will lose credibility. Transnational labor power will diminish management's ability to sustain the argument that labor relations is only a matter of local practice.

In summary, the Marxist, liberal-functionalist, and minor impact views each reflect conceptual frameworks and indicate their normative biases. The Marxist sees the MNC as imperialist and exploitative—a challenge to the trade union movement. The liberal-functionalist will seek accommodation, whereas the minor impact adherent is essentially antilabor. All of these offer a normative approach for research; however, they do not satisfactorily solve the problem of how to handle empirical data and how to determine the extent of labor transnationally as a result of MNC growth.

We must now ask if the MNC literature can be utilized to fill the gaps in the integration literature. As integration literature is concerned with the transnationality of labor relations as an issue area, the approaches of each MNC school may prove fruitful for research.

## METHODOLOGY

As noted previously, the central questions of this research are how much have coordination and cooperation occurred between labor unions transnationally within Western Europe, primarily the EEC, and what are the implications of this on the nation-state? To determine the specific extent of this coordination, a questionnaire was developed and distributed to trade unions, international trade secretariats, and other international labor bodies in Europe and the United States. Questions were asked concerning the type of cooperation between labor unions, that is, whether it was of an active nature (sympathy strikes, joint collective bargaining, and so on) or of a passive nature (exchanging information, consultation, and so on). Was this cooperation of a transnational nature, and was it specifically directed against an MNC? Moreover, unions were queried about specific bargaining tactics as well as issues that would be of mutual interest transnationally. A number of MNCs were also questioned about the extent of transnational union cooperation against themselves. In addition, position papers and strategy plans obtained from trade unions were reviewed to determine the long-range transnational strategy of these bodies.

The question of controlling variables must be addressed. It is difficult to distinguish the motivation for transnational labor response; that is, is it a product of economic integration within the EEC or MNC growth? To some extent, it is a function of both. However, it would be extremely difficult to test the data against nonintegrated areas or national companies. Thus it will be assumed that both integration and MNC development have an impact on each other and, in turn, upon labor response.

The empirical data from the questionnaires will be a measure of what has actually happened against the standard of what trade unions are stating as immediate objectives in their internal strategy documents. A number of interviews were also held with people knowledgeable about the international trade union movement, and these data will be considered with the documents related to trade union strategy.

Both the communications and neofunctionalist schools of political integration will be utilized. This will be further discussed in Chapter 2. However, it should be noted that the questionnaire has been designed as a means of measuring transactions across national borders. This is essentially the method prescribed by the communications school.

## NOTES

1. The literature in all of these areas is extensive. A few of the general major works are Herbert C. Kelman, *International Behavior: A Social-Psychological Analysis* (New York: Holt, Rinehart and Winston, for the Society for the Psychological Study of Social Issues, 1965); Joseph S. Nye, Jr., ed., *International Regionalism: Readings* (Boston: Little, Brown, under the auspices of the Center for International Affairs, Harvard University, 1968; Michael J. Brenner, *Technocratic Politics and the Functionalist Theory of European*

*Integration,* Cornell Research Papers in International Studies, no. 7 (Ithaca, N.Y.: Cornell University Press, 1969); Bruce M. Resset, *International Regions and the International System: A Study in Political Ecology,* Series in Comparative Government and International Politics (Chicago: Rand McNally, 1967); and Michael Brecher, B. Steinberg, and J. Stein, "A Framework for Research on Foreign Policy Behavior," *Journal of Conflict Resolution* 13, no. 1 (March 1969): 75–101. On Western Europe, see Ernst B. Haas, *The Unity of Europe: Political, Social and Economic Forces, 1950–1957* (Stanford, Calif.: Stanford University Press, 1958); B. Hughes and J. Schwarz, "Dimensions of Political Integration and the Experience of the EEC," *International Studies Quarterly* 16, no. 3 (September 1972): pp. 263–94; L. Lindberg, *The Political Dynamics of European Economic Integration* (Stanford, Calif.: Stanford University Press, 1963); and L. Lindberg and S. A. Scheingold, *Europe's Would-Be Polity* (Englewood Cliffs, N.J.: Prentice-Hall, 1970). On Latin America, see (on the Andean Common Market) W. Avery, "The Extra-Regional Transfer of Integrative Behavior," *International Organization* (Autumn 1973): pp. 549–56; and G. Connell-Smith, *The Inter-American System* (New York: Oxford University Press, 1966). In Ernst B. Haas, "The Study of Regional Integration," in *Regional Integration: Theory and Research,* ed. L. Lindberg and S. A. Scheingold (Cambridge, Mass.: Harvard University Press, 1971), p. 3, Haas states, "For an exhaustive list of documents relating to economic cooperation in the third world see Miguel S. Wionczeck (ed.), *Economic Cooperation in Latin America, Africa and Asia* (Cambridge: MIT Press, 1969)," p. 9.

2. Ernst B. Haas, *The Unity of Europe* (Stanford, Calif.: Stanford University Press, 1958).

3. Karl W. Deutsch, *The Analysis of International Relations* (Englewood Cliffs, N.J.: Prentice-Hall, 1968); Karl W. Deutsch, *Nationalism and Its Alternatives* (New York: Knopf, 1969); Karl W. Deutsch, *The Nerves of Government* (New York: Free Press, 1965); Karl W. Deutsch, "Security Communities," in *International Politics and Foreign Policy,* ed. James Rosenau (New York: Free Press, 1961), p. 98.

4. Carl J. Friedrich, *Trends of Federalism in Theory and Practice* (New York: Praeger, 1968), as quoted by Haas in "The Study of Regional Integration." Haas notes that federalists are divided into various camps "but they share a concern with the primary importance to institutions and their development"—thus their stress on locus of power in a federal context. See p. 20.

5. Deutsch, *Nationalism and Its Alternatives.*

6. Mitrany, according to Deutsch *(Nationalism and Its Alternatives),* envisaged the treatment of international or supranational functions as technical matters removed from interest group pressure. For further information, see David Mitrany, *A Working Peace System* (Chicago: Quadrangle, 1966).

7. Joseph S. Nye, "Patterns and Catalysts in Regional Integration," in *International Regionalism: Readings,* ed. Joseph S. Nye (Boston: Little, Brown, 1968), pp. 333–49.

8. Amatai Etzioni, *Studies in Social Change* (New York: Holt, Rinehart and Winston, 1966).

9. Haas, *The Uniting of Europe.*

10. Lindberg, *The Political Dynamics of European Economic Integration.*

11. S. A. Scheingold, *The Rule of Law in European Integration: The Path of the Schuman Plan* (New Haven, Conn.: Yale University Press, 1965).

12. Lindberg and Scheingold, *Europe's Would-Be Polity.*

13. David Easton, *A Framework for Political Analysis* (Englewood Cliffs, N.J.: Prentice-Hall, 1965).

14. Brecher, Steinberg, and Stein, "A Framework for Research on Foreign Policy Behavior"; Michael Brecher, *The Foreign Policy System of Israel: Setting, Images, Process* (New Haven, Conn.: Yale University Press, 1972), Ch. 1, pp. 1–22.

15. Stanley B. Hoffman, *Contemporary Theory in International Relations* (Englewood Cliffs, N.J.: Prentice-Hall, 1960); Stanley B. Hoffman, "International Relations: The Long Road to Theory," in *International Politics and Foreign Policy*, ed. J. Rosenau (New York: Free Press, 1961), pp. 421ff.

16. Morton Kaplan, *System and Process in International Politics* (Stanford: Stanford University Press, 1958).

17. Richard Rosecrance, *Action and Reaction in World Politics* (Boston: Little, Brown, 1963).

18. Kaplan, *System and Process in International Politics.*

19. Brecher, Steinberg, and Stein, "A Framework for Research on Foreign Policy Behavior."

20. Kaplan, *System and Process in International Politics.*

21. Haas, *Regional Integration*, p. 28.

22. Haas, *Beyond the Nation-State*, p. 92.

23. See Haas, "The Study of Regional Integration," p. 4.

24. Haas, *Beyond the Nation-State*, p. 92.

25. Deutsch, *Nationalism and Its Alternatives*, p. 99.

26. Deutsch, *The Analysis of International Relations*, p. 159.

27. Ibid.

28. Donald Puchala, "International Transactions and Regional Integration," in *Regional Integration: Theory and Research*, ed. L. Lindberg and S. A. Scheingold (Cambridge, Mass.: Harvard University Press, 1971).

29. Donald Puchala, "The Pattern of Contemporary Regional Integration," *International Studies Quarterly* 12, no. 1 (March 1968): 38–64.

30. Ibid., p. 41.

31. Ibid.

32. Ibid.

33. Puchala, "International Transactions," pp. 129 ff.

34. Ibid., p. 152.

35. Ibid.

36. Deutsch, *The Analysis of International Relations*, pp. 196–98.

37. Ibid., p. 198.

38. Ibid., p. 196.

39. Ibid., p. 198.

40. P. C. Schmitter, "A Revised Theory of Regional Integration," in *Regional Integration: Theory and Research*, ed. L. Lindberg and S. A. Scheingold (Cambridge, Mass.: Harvard University Press, 1971).

41. Ibid.

42. Ibid., p. 243.

43. Hughes and Schwarz, "Dimensions of Political Integration and the Experience of the EEC," p. 200.

44. Ibid.

45. Ibid., p. 290.

46. Ibid., p. 291.

47. Ibid.

48. Ibid.

49. L. J. Cantori and S. L. Spiegel, "The Analysis of Regional International Politics: The Integration Versus the Empirical Systems Approach," *International Organization* 27, no. 4 (Autumn 1973): 466.

50. Ibid.

51. Ibid., p. 474.

52. L. Lindberg and S. A. Scheingold, eds., *Regional Integration: Theory and Research* (Cambridge, Mass.: Harvard University Press, 1971), p. 232.

53. Ibid.

54. A. Etzioni, "The Epigenesis of Communities," p. 30.

55. Ibid., p. 41.

56. Ibid., p. 35.

57. Ibid., p. 40.

58. C. Bergsten, Robert O. Keohane, and Joseph S. Nye, "International Economics and International Politics: A Framework for Analysis," *International Organization* 29 (Winter 1975): 3–36.

59. Ibid., p. 10.

60. Joseph S. Nye, "Comparing Common Markets," in Lindberg and Scheingold, *Regional Integration.*

61. Ibid.

62. Ibid.

63. Ibid., p. 199.

64. Ibid., p. 204.

65. Ibid., p. 205.

66. Ibid., p. 212.

67. Lindberg and Scheingold, *Europe's Would-Be Polity.*

68. Ibid., p. 79.

69. Ibid.

70. Ibid., p. 65.

71. Ibid., p. 73.

72. Ibid.

73. Easton, *A Framework for Political Analysis.*

74. Brecher, *The Foreign Policy System of Israel.*

75. Brecher, Steinberg, and Stein, "A Framework for Research on Foreign Policy Behavior."

76. Brecher is indebted to, among others, Morton Kaplan, who postulated nine "systems" or configurations of world power; Richard Rosecrance, who introduced a systemic view of world history, including transformation variables indicating criteria for systemic change in *Action and Reaction in World Politics;* and Stanley Hoffman for his global views on a number of issues, including international law in "International Law and the Control of Force," in *The Relevance of International Law,* ed. Karl Deutsch and Stanley Hoffman (Cambridge, Mass.: Schenkman, 1968).

77. Gabriel A. Almond and G. Powell, *Comparative Politics: A Developmental Approach* (Boston: Little Brown, 1966).

78. Ibid.

79. Brecher, "The Middle East Subordinate System," in *Foreign Policy System of Israel: Setting, Images, Process* (New Haven, Conn.: Yale University Press, 1972), pp. 47–64.

80. Brecher, Steinberg, and Stein, "A Framework for Research on Foreign Policy."

81. Brecher, *The Foreign Policy System of Israel.*

82. Major works on the psychological dimension as applied to integration theory include H. Guetzkow, "Isolation and Collaboration: A Political Theory of Inter-National Relations," in *International Politics and Foreign Policy,* ed. J. Rosenau (New York: Free Press, 1961), pp. 152 ff.; H. Guetzkow and J. Sawyer, "Bargaining and Negotiating in International Relations," in *International Behavior: A Social-Psychological Analysis,* ed. H. C. Kelman (New York: Holt, Rinehart and Winston, 1966), pp. 464 ff.; Chadwick F. Alger, "Personal Contact in Intergovernmental Organizations," in *International Behavior: A Social-Psychological Analysis,* ed. H. C. Kelman (New York: Holt, Rinehart and

Winston, 1966), pp. 521 ff.; and J. D. Singer, ed., *Human Behavior and International Politics* (Chicago: Rand McNally, 1965).

83. Leon Lundberg and Stuart Sheingold *Regional Integration: Theory and Research* (Cambridge: Harvard University Press, 1971), p. 207.

84. Ibid., p. 212.

85. Ibid., p. 218.

86. Haas, *Beyond the Nation State.*

87. Helen Feldstein, "A Study of Transaction and Political Integration: Transnational Labour Flow Within the EEC," *Journal of Common Market Studies* (September 1967): 24–55.

88. Haas, *Beyond the Nation State.*

89. Feldstein, "A Study of Transaction and Political Integration," p. 24.

90. Ibid., p. 25.

91. See Haas, "The Study of Regional Integration," as quoted by Feldstein, p. 25.

92. Ibid.

93. Ibid., p. 46.

94. Ibid., p. 48.

95. Ibid., p. 43.

96. Joseph S. Nye, "Multinational Corporations in World Politics," *Foreign Affairs* (October 1974): 156.

97. Gabriel A. Almond and J. Coleman, eds., *The Politics of the Developing Areas* (Princeton, N.J.: Princeton University Press, 1960), pp. 3–64.

98. Haas, "The Study of Regional Integration."

99. Karl Marx and Friedrich Engels, *The Communist Manifesto,* ed. S. H. Beer (New York: Appleton Century Crofts, 1955), p. 11.

100. Ibid., p. 13.

101. Ibid., p. 19.

102. V. I. Lenin, *Imperialism, The Highest Stage of Capitalism* (New York: International Publishers, 1939), p. 109.

103. Ibid., p. 11.

104. André Gorz, *Strategy for Labor: A Radical Proposal,* trans. from the French by Martin A. Nicolaus and V. Ortiz (Boston: Beacon Press, 1967), p. 169.

105. Ibid., p. 23.

106. Hans Gunter, "An Overview of Some Recent Research on Multinational Corporations and Labour," published privately for the International Institute for Labour Studies, p. 44.

107. David H. Blake, "The Internationalisation of Industrial Relations," *Journal of International Business Studies* 3, no. 2 (Fall 1972): 17–33.

108. Duane Kujawa, *International Labor Relations Management in the Automobile Industry: A Comparative Study of Chrysler, Ford and General Motors* (New York: Praeger, 1971).

109. John Crispo, *International Unionism: A Study in Canadian-American Relations* (Toronto: McGraw-Hill, 1967).

110. Blake, "The Internationalisation of Industrial Relations."

111. Howard V. Perlmutter, "Towards Research on and Development of Nations, Unions and Firms as World-wide Institutions," in *Transnational Industrial Relations. The Impact of Multinational Corporations and Economic Regionalism to Industrial Relations,* ed. Hans Gunter (New York: Macmillan/St. Martin's Press, 1972), pp. 21–50.

112. Gunter, "An Overview of Some Recent Research on Multinational Corporations and Labour."

113. Charles Levinson, *International Trade Unionism* (London: Allen & Unwin, 1972).

114. See especially K. W. Wedderburn, "Multinational Enterprises and National Labour Law," *Industrial Law Journal* 1, no. 1 (November 1972): 12–19.

115. See R. O. Clarke, "The Multinational Company: The State and International Organizations," paper presented at the Third World Congress of the International Industrial Relations Research Association, London, September 3–7, 1973.

116. Perlmutter, "Towards Research on and Development of Nations, Unions and Firms as World-wide Institutions."

117. Hans Gunter, "The Future of Transnational Industrial Relations: A Tentative Framework for Analysis," in *Transnational Industrial Relations. The Impact of Multinational Corporations and Economic Regionalism to Industrial Relations,* ed. Hans Gunter (New York: Macmillan/St. Martin's Press, 1972), p. 427.

118. Ibid.

119. Perlmutter, "Towards Research on and Development of Nations, Unions and Firms as World-wide Institutions."

120. Gunter, "The Future of Transnational Industrial Relations," p. 429.

121. Ibid., p. 430.

122. Perlmutter, "Towards Research on and Development of Nations, Unions and Firms as World-wide Institutions."

123. Ibid., p. 27.

124. Ibid., p. 41.

125. Ibid., p. 47.

126. Gunter, "An Overview of Some Recent Research on Multinational Corporations and Labour," p. 41.

127. Ibid., p. 43.

128. H. Northrup and R. Rowan, "Multinational Collective Bargaining Activity: The Factual Record in Chemicals, Glass, and Rubber Tires. Pt. II," *Columbia Journal of World Business* (Summer 1974): 49–62.

129. Ibid., p. 60.

130. W. Curtin and I. Shepard, "International Labor Relations: Multinational Collective Bargaining—an Illusory Concept," *Employee Relations Law Journal* 1, no. 1 (Summer 1975): 128–48.

131. D. Lea, "Multinational Companies and Trade Union Interests," in *The Multinational Enterprise,* ed. J. H. Dunning (New York: Praeger, 1971), p. 147.

132. D. Barran, "Comment on the Chapter by Mr. Lea: A Businessman's Viewpoint," in *The Multinational Enterprise,* ed by J. H. Dunning (New York: Praeger, 1971), p. 164.

133. Barnet and Muller, *Global Reach.* For further comments on the management perspective, see B. C. Roberts, "Factors Influencing the Organisation and Style of Management and Their Effect on the Pattern of Industrial Relations in Multinational Corporations," *Transnational Industrial Relations. The Impact of Multinational Corporations and Economic Regionalism to Industrial Relations,* ed. Hans Gunter (New York: St. Martin's Press, 1972), pp. 109–32.

# 2 THE INTERNATIONAL STRATEGY OF THE TRADE UNION

The essence of industrial relations for both management and labor is the development of a coordinated and soundly prepared strategy. The capability of a true geocentric multinational in Howard Perlmutter's sense to develop strategy is, by definition, according to R. J. Barnet and R. E. Muller, "global."[1] How have the unions responded to this development? In what sense and to what degree does the trade union movement have a "global" strategy to deal with the growth and "geocentrizing" of multinational corporations? This chapter will review data given by union officials in Europe and the United States detailing their multinational strategy. Note that to a large extent the data represent union claims which—although attempted—was difficult to verify at company sources.

Trade unions have released a body of literature explaining their case against the multinational. Their basic argument can be summarized as the following:

1. Multinationals avoid taxation. "Transfer pricing is quite simply robbery" according to the Postal International Trade Secretariat.[2] Unions are concerned with the MNCs' ability to shift income reports between national profit centers to avoid taxation. Thus income reported to a national government may not truly reflect national profit. Because unions traditionally negotiate on a national basis, they are at a major disadvantage when set against the ability of the MNC to sustain losses.

As collective bargaining occurs at the national level, it becomes extremely difficult to determine wage and benefit increases that are truly reflective of a company's ability to pay. Unions argue that MNCs reduce their national income statements for collective bargaining purposes. Thus income produced in a country is often shifted outside to reduce taxes and concurrently to diminish trade union demands upon national corporate revenue.

The World Conferederation of Labor, (organized originally as a group of confessional unions) has declared that "the MNC's dispose of large 'floating' liquidities and this in multiple currencies ... they have mobility sufficient to permit them making the financial operations which are the most interesting at their point of view ... they are not submitted to the constraints of the governments policies of credit"[3]

2. Multinational planning does not account for and may be inimical to the national economy. Projections and programs are not integrated into national planning and do not coincide with the self-interest of the nation-state. The International Confederation of Free Trade Unions (ICFTU) has noted that "Europeans not only provide considerable funds on the spot to help American firms set up and run their subsidiaries in Europe, but also transfer across the Atlantic a lot of their spare cash, which thus becomes available to American big business for further direct investment in Europe or elsewhere."[4]

The ICFTU has been a major proponent of integrating corporate and national planning. It speaks for most of the "liberal" trade unions in the noncommunist West. Although the ICFTU does not have the bargaining power of an industrial trade secretariat, its primary influence is through position platforms to which national trade unions adhere. There are 123 affiliate organizations in 95 countries belonging to the ICFTU, including the AFL-CIO in the United States, the Trades Union Congress in the United Kingdom, and the Confederation of German Trade Unions (DGB) in Germany. Representation is approximately 63 million workers, compared to 160 million affiliated with the World Federation of Trade Unions (Communist countries) and 16 million in the World Confederation of Labor (Christian National Trade Union Centers).[5] Thus, when the ICFTU indicates that, "there is no control or integration of their [MNC] corporate policy within national and economic goals" ... it can be assumed that a broad component of the international trade union movement is being spoken for. The ICFTU goes on to state, "With the growing dependence of world trade and technological development on MNC's such decisions are already beginning to determine the nature of economic activity."[6]

3. Multinationals do not always generate the maximum level of employment. The Postal International Trade Secretariat has indicated that "countries with high unemployment have frequently found that investment by an MNC has not generated the volume of employment which might have been produced by the same fund in a different way —and the reason has usually been the MNC's choice of technology, and not that which suited the real needs of the society."[7] The net effect of

this argument, if true, is that certain skills requiring a high degree of training can be bid away by an MNC in a less developed work force leaving a skill scarcity. Minimal impact is made upon reducing unemployment.[8]

4. Multinationals have little understanding of local ways of doing business and seek to export their own foreign headquarters. This charge has been levied primarily against U.S. firms. The British Trades Union Congress's study on international companies states that "it is suggested that these companies [MNCs] were typical of all foreign-owned subsidiaries, but certain attitudes towards trade unionism do emerge, particularly with the U.S.-owned firms." This in part reflects the situation in the U.S.A., where only 22 percent of the labor force is unionized, as against 42 percent in the United Kingdom. Firms in the United States operate at home under the National Labor Relations Board (NLRB) regulations and are accustomed to delaying recognition until they are legally obligated to by elections conducted by the NLRB. This contrasts with the "voluntarism" of British industrial relations.[9]

An adversary relationship is acceptable to both management and labor in the United States. It is the basic premise of the U.S. style of collective bargaining. Furthermore, the emphasis upon NLRB elections implies that management campaigns to avoid union organization are an acceptable business practice. The export of the U.S.-style adversary relationship between management and labor is frequently raised as an issue by European trade unionists. They see accommodation or, more lately, comanagement as the only acceptable relationship between unions and MNCs. Thus the basic U.S. style of labor relations in the United Kingdom and Europe is contrary to traditional practice there.

Specifically, this style can be noted in the following instances where union avoidance occurred by a U.S.-based MNC in Europe:

1. *Kodak.* Kodak attempted to establish its own "worker representation committees." This was perceived as a management device to counter unions, and subsequently the Transport and General Workers Union organized Kodak by gaining membership on the committee.
2. *Roberts Arundel.* This U.S.-based textile company refused recognition of the Engineering and Foundry Workers when a small machinery company was purchased in the United Kingdom. A 12-month strike ensued, and the plant was subsequently closed.
3. *Caterpillar Tractor.* This company refused to recognize a union incursion. A strike lasted 13 weeks with the end result being union recognition.
4. IBM, Gillette, H. J. Heinz, and Fairchild have all had union recognition disputes.

Nonrecognition of unions, while a standard U.S. procedure, is not common in the United Kingdom. Indeed, recognition is so acceptable that legal machinery to do this was not established until 1971 when the short-lived Industrial Relations Act was passed. The objective was to "bring order" to industrial relations. Its demise can be attributed to union pressure and the unions' inability to live with what was viewed as a restrictive framework. It is accepted that management will deal with a union once a group of workers request this.

IBM and Kodak in particular are known to be difficult to organize even in countries where union organization is virtually ubiquitous. If recognition is achieved, these and other U.S. firms have a reputation for avoiding employers associations, which represent management at national contract negotiations. In the United Kingdom, Exxon is not a member of the Employers Panel of the oil companies' Conciliation Committee. Thus another U.S.-style tactic—company or local level bargaining—as opposed to the European practice of industrywide bargaining, has been attempted by American MNCs, according to international unionists.

Multinationals have the ability to switch production to another country. This perhaps is the ultimate threat that an MNC has. In effect, an MNC can tell a union that, if pressed too hard, it will go out of business and start anew where labor demands will be lessened. The most publicized example of this is Henry Ford's threat to leave the United Kingdom (announced after a meeting with Prime Minister Edward Heath) in 1970 if the industrial relations climate did not significantly improve. Ford was not solely concerned with the U.K. company but all of Ford-Europe. Unlike General Motors, Ford is highly integrated within Europe. Thus Europeanwide integration of production not only maximized efficiency but also increased vulnerability to work stoppages. In effect, transnational production lines must come to a halt if components from one nation are not received by another.

In 1969, Ford terminated 1,500 employees in Genk, Belgium, because of a strike at a U.K. plant. The "management of the Cologne plant made similar statements that in the future they did not want to be dependent on British components."[10] Charles Levinson, head of the International Chemical Workers Federation, indicates that although an agreement was reached with Ford, it was not reflective of the union membership's wishes. This is because a significant section of the agreement involving penal clauses was ratified by a small union executive body. A new work stoppage then resulted with the objective of reforming the negotiating structure by giving a larger voice to majority union and shop stewards.[11] Thus the international trade secretariat's reaction to the Ford strike was one of attempting to democratize the work place at a moment when Ford Motor Company was particularly vulnerable.

The Ford issue is one which could have been highly detrimental to the U.K. economy if the company had pulled out production facilities. It was primarily pressure from the U.K. government and the acquiescence of the unions—and, of course, the major plant investment—that made Ford decide to stay. A similar scenario has been played at Chrysler U.K. What is important to note at this point is that the threat of large MNCs to shift production facilities or to move production by either increasing employment or overtime to another country is a new form of leverage against trade unions.

Henry Ford realized that the instability of the U.K. labor environment could cause disruption throughout Europe. Thus, by threatening to remove jobs from the United Kingdom, he was playing upon a perceived lack of Europeanwide labor unity. Sufficient Europeanwide coordination could negate the potential impact of Ford's threatened move from the United Kingdom. Workers in Belgium, Germany, and so on could join in a work stoppage if Ford left the United Kingdom. What happened, however, was that Ford did triumph, in the short run, and bought the United Kingdom labor peace. However, this threat was enough to coalesce European unions. This will be discussed further when the International Metalworkers Federation is examined.

Decision-making activity rests with headquarters in a multinational, not with local management. The primary union complaint concerning collective bargaining is that MNCs are elusive and that local national management does not have the authority to enter into contracts or allocate funds. If attempts are made to go to the major decision-making center—headquarters—unions are rebuffed because it is company policy "not to interfere in local practice" or that labor relations is a national matter.

The basic premise of the international trade union MNC strategy is that the national corporate body is becoming less of a primary actor in industrial relations. The interdependence of the world economy, as well as the extraordinary growth of the multinational corporation, produces a necessity for transnational trade union linkage. These transnational ties, through international trade union bodies, as well as informal links, indicate a trend that international trade union action must be the primary means of effective industrial relations.

The trade union response to these six issues can be viewed on a continuum of international industrial action (to be discussed in detail in Chapter 3). It ranges from the exchange of information to joint collective bargaining and sympathy strikes across national borders. The strategy has been the result of both long-range planning by trade unions and transnational ad hoc meetings on specific issues.

Formal positions on multinationals have been taken by at least five of the sixteen international trade secretariats as well as national trade union centers in numerous countries, for example, the Trades Union Congress in the United Kingdom and the Lands organisation (LOs: national centers) of Norway, Sweden, and Denmark. To some extent this is remarkable when one views the organizational difficulties that place limitations upon developing a coherent viewpoint. Although all positions have a common thread, each of them is quite specific to meet the circumstances of its region or country. Positions also vary depending upon whether it is an international or national trade union center in question. At this juncture, these positions will be examined. Discussion will not be held on a country-by-country basis, but on either a country or organizational (ITS) level, depending upon the source of the MNC trade union position.

## COUNCIL OF NORDIC TRADE UNIONS

The NFS, or Council of Nordic Trade Unions, represents the five national worker trade union centers of Denmark, Finland, Iceland, Norway, and Sweden, as well as three national salaried trade union centers from these countries. A meeting was held in Finland in 1974 to establish a program for dealing with multinationals.

Scandinavian unions traditionally have maintained close ties as a result of the development of companies based in these countries, most notably SAS (the Scandinavian Airlines System). Furthermore, the acceptance of the concept of codetermination in both Sweden and Norway with active participation through the trade unions has made unions extremely powerful. The centralization of trade unions through a national center has made a transnational coordinating point easier to develop than in countries where trade unions are divided by ideological or religious national centers. The development of pioneering autonomous work groups, particularly in Norway and Sweden, has also fostered closer ties among the workers of these countries. However, it was not until 1974 that a formal position was established on multinationals, although there had been informal communications on the "problem" for some time.

The NFS has declared that it will seek a number of means to reduce the influence of foreign-based MNCs in "order to improve the possibilities of control and to eliminate the various risks arising from an extensive foreign influence over the economies of the Nordic countries."[12] It proposes to do this by legislating prior government authorization for foreign-based investment. In the event of large takeovers, mergers, and acquisitions, the state would have the right to "total or partial owner-ship if it so opted," and most importantly, this authorization would not be granted unless "the employees have total insight into the accounts and the policy of the firm."[13] To deal with the issue of transfer pricing, the NFS proposes that uniform legislation in each country prohibit this and that "the calculation of the income of the different units of a same group shall be based on the total profit of the group."

A major concern of trade unions is the legal prohibition in some countries of international sympathy action, for example, the United Kingdom and the five Nordic countries. The NFS has specifically sought to obtain this right through joint pressure on its national legisla-tures. Transnational sympathy strikes, political strikes, and boycotts where presently not authorized are all viewed as legally desirable and a significant tactic for transnational labor action against MNCs.

The NFS justifies its actions not only for the self-interest of the workers but also because of the harm it believes MNCs are causing the state. The impact of MNCs, in its view, has been a "process of interna-tionalization . . . threatening to reduce the fiscal resources of the states to the point of seriously jeopardizing their ability to meet their national and social obligations."[14]

Other position papers, including the one by the AFL-CIO, refer to the negative impact on the national economy an MNC may have as it affects them, that is, unemployment; however, only the NFS expresses concern about national integrity.* This may explain the Scandinavian Trade Union's emphasis upon control through national legislation rather than boycotts, international strikes, and so forth. These latter tactics are, of course, pressed, and certainly they would actively engage in such activity when called upon to do so by other national unions, but it cannot be disregarded that the major emphasis is on national legisla-tion.

The unity of the Nordic area from a trade union viewpoint will be more closely examined in the questionnaire data; however, at this point, it can be stated that it is the only region in Europe that has an active and formal program for trade union actions against the MNC.

---

*The formulation of AFL-CIO policy is essentially through George Meany and his council of international representatives. Irving Brown has been the AFL-CIO "ambassa-dor" to Europe for years and has a very strong voice in formulation of international policy. The questionnaire response that I received was signed by Michael Boggs of the International Department.

## THE UNITED KINGDOM: TRADES UNION CONGRESS

The major Trades Union Congress (TUC) position paper is "Report of a Conference on International Companies," which contains the proceedings of a meeting held in October 1970. Since that time, there has been discussion not only of international action but also of worker participation or, as it is called in the United Kingdom, "industrial democracy."[15] The TUC does note that the ability of national governments to control their own economies is "severely undermined"[16] because the "international company is rapidly replacing the nation-state as the basic operating and accounting unit in the international economy."[17] The uniqueness of the United Kingdom is that it is "both a parent on a large scale of international companies and a recipient of large scale inward investment by overseas companies."[18]

The TUC set forth the following position:

1. to set up a systematic collection of information on British and foreign-owned international companies operating in the United Kingdom,
2. to put pressure on government to enforce, by a new Companies Act, disclosure of more information on the activities of international companies regarding the relation of the United Kingdom to global activities,
3. to put pressure on the government to ensure that international companies taking over United Kingdom firms are fully apprised of their industrial relations responsibilities, and
4. to develop increased consultation between international companies operating in the United Kingdom and British trade unions on corporate planning.[19]

The TUC further proposed that it would work with international trade secretariats to obtain information on corporate decision-making processes, finance, and so on, and to lend mutual support (by means of banning overtime, prevention of production switches, sympathy strikes, and so forth).

Since the proposal of this resolution, the Industrial Relations Act has been passed and replaced by the Employment Protection Act, the first viewed by British labor as an attempt to impose severe legal constraints by a Conservative government, the latter as a modified form of the same, only this time with party support. The TUC has developed an extensive information-exchange system and has pushed for control of all companies, but primarily MNCs, through codetermination or worker representation on company boards. The original objection to codetermination by the TUC was that representation was viewed as a threat to trade unionism if nonunion workers could serve on a board. The TUC is now willing to support it as long as representation is through the unions.

To a great extent, the TUC position on MNCs has been precipitated by the refusal of Kodak, IBM, and Roberts Arundel to recognize unions and to conform with United Kingdom industrial relations practices. When Kodak attempted to establish its own form of worker representation as a means of thwarting unions, the Transport and General Workers Union covertly gained membership on the board and organized the company. The National Union of Journalists was particularly adamant about the organization of Kodak. It said: "It is a ridiculous situation when an industry such as publishing is very unionized—up to 100% in the craft trades—should be largely dependent on the photographers side on a priority supplier which has a company union."[20]

The Journalists Union's complaint in essence concerned the impact of U.S. monopoly's practices on the United Kingdom way of doing business and the export of U.S. industrial relations practices.[21] The reaction of Kodak—company-sponsored "worker participation"—was seen as a major effort to usurp U.K. industrial relations practice.

Clive Jenkins, president of the Association of Scientific, Technical and Managerial Staffs (ASTMS) has been extremely active in the development of a transnational labor movement. He has pitted his union against foreign-based MNCs in the financial (white-collar) industry, and has indicated that the most effective tactic is to begin with Western European collective bargaining. Jenkins states, "We are talking in terms of great MNC's, manufacturing or extracting corporations, in terms of those with a power base in the U.S. and, less importantly, those with a power base in Holland, West Germany, Sweden and the U.K.... I think we are going to have to think of collective bargaining at least on a Western European basis."[22]

There have been reports that Jenkins' union (membership 850,000) "is moving firmly into the international arena."[23] Jenkins refused to support the recent U.K. subsidy to Chrysler U.K. because of objections to "redundancy" or layoff provisions. ASTMS managed to obtain meetings with Chrysler officials in Detroit to "coordinate future trade union policy." Indeed, meetings were also held in Detroit by trade union officials from France who represented employees from Chrysler's Simca. It should be noted however, that one sees little, if any, concrete results from these meetings.

Jenkins believes that Western European collective bargaining will develop as a result of the United Kingdom's entry into the EEC.[24] The TUC issued a report indicating that, as a result of entry into the EEC, the practice of codetermination as practiced on the Continent could be adapted to the United Kingdom. This is an alternative to direct organizing of such companies as Kodak and would permit union representation and formal transnational communication among worker delegates on a multinational board. The TUC has thus opted to pressure for two-tier boards through union representation. This is a modification of the German system. At the EEC level, the TUC is also pressuring for a European company law whereby MNCs would register as European companies. "In the specific case of European-level machinery in the suggested European company, as far as British plants are concerned this would need to be on trade union machinery. The aim would be to give some multinational union control over those MNC decisions."[25]

In summary, the TUC position has been to collect and coordinate information on MNCs, to press for the legalization of international sympathy strikes and boycotts, to work with international trade secretariats on transnational bargaining where appropriate, and to adopt worker participation as a means of combatting U.S.-style industrial relations. Collective bargaining, especially at the local plant level, will remain the primary cornerstone of U.K. labor relations, but the TUC is willing to join with Western Europe on codetermination as a means of controlling multinationals.

## INTERNATIONAL CONFEDERATION OF FREE TRADE UNIONS

Trade unions are all nationally based. However, "national trade unions do achieve an international scope through affiliation with two other kinds of organizations whose activities are fundamentally multinational: the International Trade Secretariats and the International Confederations of Trade Unions."[26] As previously noted, there are 16 ITSs whose primary function is to coordinate national unions at the employer level and on an industrywide basis. The confederation groups national centers (TUC, AFL-CIO, and so on) and deals primarily with legislative problems through international bureaucracies, for example, OECD, UN, or EEC. Although they have been less active in creating direct transnational ties, they have created an environment for transnational labor activity. The ICFTU, representing the bulk of "free world" unions (the World Confederation of Labor having the rest), has been especially active at the European level through its offshoot, the European Trade Union Confederation although there are currently no formal ties between these two organizations.

The ICFTU in its official statement, "The Multinational Challenge" (September 1971), set the framework for action by its affiliates. It provided a list of companies refusing to deal with unions by establishing collective bargaining procedures. General Motors and Remington were particularly noted for head-office decision making and for dismissals in France without local consultation. Raytheon and Muller Wupperthorth were also accused of similar actions in Italy.

The ICFTU position is that, "in the absence of coordinated international trade union action, it tips the balance of bargaining power in favor of management against labor."[27] The ICFTU has served as a forum for the national trade union centers to exchange information. The German Metalworkers Federation was one of the original proponents for ICFTU coordination as a means of combatting "the different levels of labor costs ... frequently used by the employers to play the trade unions off against one another. ... This policy of trying to sow dissent in our ranks must be encountered with a firm and consistent approach —intensification of exchange of information."[28] At the same conference in which this discussion occurred (1969), it was decided that the jurisdiction of the confederations would be to deal with MNCs on the questions of tax-dodging, currency manipulation, and "sowers of dissension," whereas the ITSs would deal with the exploitation issue.[29] In practice there has been overlapping. The major action taken by the ICFTU has been to press for a multinational code of conduct. It appears that it is nearing success.

The OECD ratified a multinational code of conduct in June 1976. It is the result of both business and trade union recommendations. The Trade Union Advisory Council (TUAC) of the OECD has had significant ICFTU data input. The trade union body has pressed for full financial disclosure for collective bargaining purposes. The proposal "would require MNC's to furnish information on corporate structure, including the size of the parents' shareholdings in group subsidiaries and the extent of cross-participation in companies affiliated with the group."[30] MNC investment activity on a national basis would have to be disclosed as well as the size of the payroll in each country.

The OECD Code has been supported in principle by Xerox. M. Thomas, chairman of Rank Xerox (U.K.), has stated that a multinational charter would be a positive development. He has proposed an MNC council to act "as a bridge between such international institutions as the U.N., EEC and International Chamber of Commerce."[31] Of course, this response could be viewed as a means of thwarting the proposals set forth by the TUAC in the OECD recommendations.*

The ICFTU has strongly opposed the spread of MNCs to the third world and socialist countries. Although this volume is not concerned with MNC activities in the third world, it should be noted that alleged exploitation in that area has been a major criticism by trade unions: "They suspect that multinational firms with a long and obstinate record of opposing the organization of their employees into unions—and their blacklist includes such giants as IBM, Kodak, United Fruit, Firestone, First National City Bank—would feel at home in a Communist country, where the trade unions are under strict state control."[32]

Charles Wright, of the Economic Office of the ICFTU, told me that their organization was especially opposed to "arrangements between national governments and MNCs." He cited "tax-free holidays," which means exemption from taxes, as an example. He also thought that in some countries there was a tacit understanding that the "labor side will not provide a problem."† This is particularly true in developing countries.

The ICFTU has attempted to initiate some action by holding a world congress every three years. Wright stated that, although the international trade secretariats were not members of the organization, they did work closely with these congresses. He stated that the ultimate objective of these congresses has been to obtain a UN agreement whereby companies are legally obligated to disclose financial data on all affiliates. National legislation has been encouraged, but there is a necessity for world agreement similar to the General Agreement on Tariffs and Trade (GATT). He believes that a permanent UN commission would police this. He said that the Trade Union Congress in the

---

*U.S. officials characterized the OECD Code as the "best deal we can get in view of the circumstances. TUAC had actively proposed international bargaining as a *standard* for MNC's." [Statement by official U.S. business representatives to BIAC (Business International Advisory Council) before the International Chamber of Commerce business briefing on the OECD Code, June 1, 1976, Washington, D.C.] This was rejected in early debate. John Neihuss of the Treasury Department explained that the original push for the OECD Code came from U.S. Treasury Secretary John Connolly, who was concerned about investment incentives in Canada. Michelin, the French tire company, had set up a plant in Newfoundland to (in Connolly's eyes) "dump" tires into the U.S. market. He asked for the OECD to review the issue and it decided to develop a code on MNCs. Canada has reluctantly agreed to the code. The United Kingdom and Sweden have also, but indicated they wished the code had gone *farther.*

†Interview with Charles Wright, Economic Office, ICFTU, Brussels, Belgium, April 1974.

United Kingdom and the DGB, the National Trade Union Center for Workers in Germany, are currently providing the primary source of research material.

Wright thought that in the future there would be a closer relationship established with the "working group" of the ICFTU and political parties. The Swedish minister of labor was invited to the last ICFTU meeting, and a representative of the socialist international was also present. Wright took particular pride in coordination by the ICFTU and the ITSs at the Farah strike in Texas in which "$10 million was lost in one quarter." The ICFTU contacted affiliates around the world, informed them of conditions at Farah, and coordinated with the Textile Workers International Secretariat, headed by Charles Ford. The result was that a consumer boycott was organized.*

## WORLD CONFEDERATION OF LABOR

Although the World Confederation of Labor (WCL) and ICFTU maintain their independence, there has been an organizational coalescing within Europe. Both WCL and ICFTU formed European regional organizations that merged in 1973 to form the European Trade Union Council (ETUC). Both the European Free Trade Association (EFTA) and EEC countries are represented. Some WCL members affiliated directly with ETUC, such as Confédéracion Francaise Democratique du Travail (CFDT) in France, the Catholic Workers (NKV) Federation in the Netherlands, and the Christian Syndicate (CSC) of Belgium. There have been major efforts by the ETUC to establish ties with the communist federation, the World Federation of Labor, based in Prague.

The WCL Congress met in September 1973 to develop a policy on multinationals. It prepared a remarkable and technical document analyzing the economic impact of MNCs, and from this developed a program. The analysis was much further to the left than the ICFTU platform, perhaps reflecting the more progressive or left socialist influence of the CFDT and NKV.

The WCL criticized MNCs for the following reasons:

1. Establishing an international division of labor. The split was seen as one between industrialized and developing countries. The ICFTU thought more in terms of MNC/home-country corporations with wage drift between the two and antiunionism by the giants. The WCL sees MNCs as consciously perpetuating an inter-

---

*Wright interview.

national division of labor that eventually, due to decreasing profits, will "transfer to the countries having a very low cost of production".[33]

2. Trade and monetary disruption. The MNC is a major speculator in the international money market causing inflation and monetary instability.

3. Political "structure." The WCL sees MNCs and the capitalist states as working in collusion. "Social peace" programs and so on are indications of this where government and business join as "partners." The international bureaucracies, GATT and ILO, for example, only support this.

The WCL position continues with statements of capitalist societies being agents for colonialism and diffusion of capitalist ideology. It points to MNC dismissal of militant trade unionists, the threat of shifting production, parallel "replacement" centers for production, and the technique of "human relations" and worker participation as being schemes to perpetuate the capitalist system at the expense of the worker. On the latter point—worker participation (codetermination)—it should be noted that both Confederazione Generale Italiana del Lavoro (CIGL) and CGT, the communist federations in Italy and France, respectively, have been opposed because it is viewed as "collaboration" with the capitalist class.

The program of the WCL is directed at both national governments and international agencies coupled with transnational coordination between unions. It, like the ICFTU and TUC, calls for prior notice to the trade unions before further national programs for investment by MNCs. It also seeks vigorous enforcement of laws prohibiting certain types of "concentration."[34] In this instance it has gone further than the ICFTU, which declares that it seek accommodation with the MNCs. The WCL seeks to break up monopoly MNCs and thus disavows the policy of accommodation.

One program stressed by the WCL (and ETUC) is international worker education. Specifically, it is stated it wants "financial possibilities given to the workers for the utilization of the paid educational holiday and to the trade unions to endow their organizations with services of survey of a technical nature and for training purposes offering to the workers."[35] The European Trade Union Congress has also encouraged an active program of educating young workers in factories about MNCs.[36]

The WCL has supported a multinational code, which, in addition to ICFTU proposals, asked for obligation of a yearly meeting (at company cost) of all of the trade union delegates of the group, minimum wage and work norms MNC-wide, and respect of the absolute priority of employment (minimum quota of national employment at all levels). The WCL wants a Court of International Law to enforce the code. It would demand that MNCs subscribe to this code in all countries where they are established.[37]

The ICFTU and WCL have gone beyond the traditional framework of collective bargaining in many countries, particularly the United States and United Kingdom. They have provided a framework and program for coping with the full impact of MNCs on the state. The issues of taxation, transfer pricing, and employment levels not only concern the immediate impact on the worker but also the broader question of state control, state power, and, by implication, state sovereignty. The two federations have taken the position that the national state is no longer capable of controlling its own economy and a major reason for this is the ability of the MNC to control resources transnationally. Thus the route to job security, employment, and higher wages and benefits must be through international action on broader issues that determine the standard "bread and butter" levels. This is the role of the World Confederation of Labor (WCL). The more immediate issues are handled by the international trade secretariats, most of which are based in Geneva.

## THE INTERNATIONAL TRADE SECRETARIATS: FIET

FIET, the International Federation of Commercial, Clerical and Technical Employees, "advocates the trend from national economies to continental economies and are not against the liberalization of world trade, as foretokened by the multinationals, as long as the proper conditions are met, any more than we are against automation or technological advances."[38] FIET focuses concern on the developing/ industrialized split. It is one of the few ITSs (I do not know of a specific reason why) that attributes world inflation primarily to MNCs and is concerned with the impact of their purchasing power—the liquid reserves MNCs have—particularly in the developing world. The relocation to lands of cheap labor, coupled with tax incentives and raw materials in the developing countries, "causes unemployment in the industrialized countries."[39]

FIET's position includes the previously described critique of MNCs; however, unlike others, it specifically mentions "their enormous capital strength to infringe the sovereignty of the host country and influence its domestic and foreign policy,"[40] MNCs therefore are more comfortable with authoritarian regimes where there are no strikes. Because primary loyalty is to shareholders and to the host country (this is the behavior of the ethnocentric MNC in Perlmutter's classification system), it is the worker who suffers the most.[41]

FIET's strategy has the following objective: "An MNC must in principle be responsible through its central management for all its workers, manual and non-manual, in every country. Profits should be considered as a whole; so should company policy, including staff policy."[42] FIET's action program has been to coordinate data gathering for bargaining sessions transnationally through its affiliated unions. Some unions have been assigned specific firms, for example, the HBV of Germany (Commerce, Banking and Insurance Companies Union—part of DGB) is working on Citibank, SBMF of Sweden (Swedish Bank Clerk Federation) is covering Lloyds Bank, and APEX (Association of Professional, Executive, Clerical and Computer Staff) of the United Kingdom will issue a report on Phillips. Thus unions have become fact gatherers and research bases for future international negotiations. Indeed, these unions have already been assigned the task of heading the negotiating committee for the companies upon which they are doing research.[43]

FIET states that it already has held discussions with the headquarters management of the Swiss insurance MNC, Winterthur. Although Winterthur saw this meeting as a lessening of local management activity, it nevertheless chose to meet about general working conditions in various countries. FIET is particularly strong in the insurance and banking industries, and thus it is not surprising that it chose an MNC in the financial area for its first "test case." "The FIET Winterthur committee, composed of one Swiss, one Belgian, one Austrian, one Swedish and two German colleagues is preparing a draft collective agreement. In our bargaining with the MNC, we must be guided by the principle that provisions must always be superior to those in force at national level."[44]

FIET therefore has major plans. It is one of the most active ITSs in transnational labor relations, and fully believes that an international collective agreement is possible. It has established sources of data collection with the objective of "targeting" specific companies. It has held one transnational meeting with a major multinational employer and has been active in consumer boycotts. One noteworthy boycott occurred in Peru against Sears Roebuck in support of the Retail Clerks International Association (RCIA). One response by the RCIA is that it "is willing to head a world committee for this company [Sears]."[45]

The RCIA is U.S.-based. Most of FIET's international efforts have been centered in Europe through EURO-FIET. The regional concept of union organization has been applied elsewhere in FIET, and it would appear that cooperation is becoming global. FIET is providing a global vehicle for transnational ties and action against MNCs by salaried employees. Part of these global efforts can be attributed to the links that FIET's leader, Heribert Maier, has with the ICFTU, having been head of ICFTU's Economic, Social and Political Department.

## INTERNATIONAL METALWORKERS FEDERATION

The IMF is considered by most observers to be among the five most active ITSs. The major studies on the IMF include that of Duane Kujawa,[46] which Nat Weinberg of the UAW (United Autoworkers) claimed was "management biased"[47] (and I generally agree), and Everett Kassalow's unpublished manuscript.[48] In addition, there are data that will be reported in this section from interviews with Nat Weinberg and Karl Casserini, an IMF official and perhaps the most eminent economist in the employ of an ITS.

Kassalow's work will be reviewed sufficiently by critics upon publication. At this juncture, it is worthwhile to reiterate his themes and conclusions because they lend insight into the development of transnational unionism vis-a-vis the MNC. Kassalow believes that because of the scope of the IMF—the broad metalworking industry—which would include both the UAW and International Association of Machinists (IAM) in the United States, the organization of the IMF into "departments" and the rapid postwar industrial growth of the EEC made it "not a very difficult step to pass to a world company council approach with councils being established first, in the early fifties, for Ford and General Motors, at the time the only significant MNC's."[49]

Thus, the world council approach that coalesced a group of unions transnationally against a specific MNC was developed in the auto industry through the IMF. Kassalow believes that councils have tended to emphasize the "business" unionism approach as opposed to "the somewhat older and more traditional European labor-socialist conceptions of socializing."[50] He attributes this to the specificity of demands that must be formulated; however, it is possible that it can be attributed to the undue influence of the big U.S. unions. Interestingly, the French and Italian unions have opposed this approach, so that a major task of multinational unionism as expressed by the IMF has been to "blend ... powerful national forces."[51]

Kassalow notes what should be considered a key determinant of the potential of transnational unionism with respect to the IMF: In "developed countries it is not the nature of the industry alone, in a given country, which has shaped the unions' roles in IMF and especially its automotive work. The make-up of a given national union, its jurisdiction, its union competition at home, the way in which it bargains, the character, all influence its role."[52] Thus the major obstacle to the world company council approach, a major innovation in transnational unionism, was the overcoming of nationalism by unions—essentially a question of jurisdiction. "Indeed, at first they only grudgingly yielded to the pressures for an auto council set up in the IMF itself. This early reluctance stemmed from their fears as to what a company council approach in IMF might do to their own bargaining structures and policies. By the mid and late sixties, most of these fears had disappeared."[53]

Specifically, the IMF has developed the most sophisticated preparations for transnational bargaining. Although the actual negotiations still occur at the national level, the argument is becoming more and more transnational. The primary example of this is indicated in a private document, "IMF Systematic Analysis of Multinational Companies Worldwide and at Subsidiary Level." As the approach is global, it links total profits to subsidiary/country net returns on investment and places accountability at headquarters instead of country management. In management's view, this is almost heretical and counter to the prevailing management view that "local practice" is the standard for the establishment of wages and working conditions. Thus the Ford report begins with noting that "it is shocking that during a time of continued cutbacks in working hours in Germany, Ford decided on a 35% dividend."[54]

The objectives of the Ford study were to present a case for multinational bargaining not only to Ford management but also to the IMF constituent bodies and to demonstrate that Ford-U.K. was not only profitable but that it was extremely unlikely that Ford would pull out of Britain. The study uses the Marxist concept of value added, defined by Casserini as "the profit earning power measured against the values of created production."[55] Value added is an effective means of comparing worker productivity between countries (in relation to gross operating profit). However, in some instances statistics are used to oversimplification, for example, when comparing value added to operating profit it is 37 percent in the United Kingdom and Germany "as against 29–½% for the world average." The conclusion from this is that "it counters any allegations of Ford management that the German or British worker is either less or more productive, or remunerative to the company. It is futile for the company to try and play off one worker against the other."[56] The fallacy is that the comparison is with the *world* average, which, of course, yields a lower base due to many factors, including lower productivity in lesser developed countries.

The IMF is on more solid ground when it discusses the integration of Ford-Europe because of the dependence between British and German Ford and "their mutual involvement in Belgium." The IMF adds the sales figures of the U.K. and German subsidiaries and divides by the total number of employees in both countries. This figure (sales per employee) is then compared to the rate of increase of sales in the remainder of Ford. The conclusion is that "the sales per employee in Europe increased almost 100% as against 38% worldwide and 50% in the U.S. and Canada."[57]

The IMF argues that productivity in both operations and sales in a consolidated form (transnational) is the most appropriate in an integrated company. Thus bargaining on the basis of national productivity or any other indicator of worker "success" does not reflect the reality of the multinational. The argument is computed, according to the IMF, when looking at export figures instead of domestic sales. Thus market share of Ford-Germany is only 11 percent; however, 70 percent of that country's production is exported.[58] The United Kingdom compensates for lack of exports by domestic market—27 percent. This is the same as North America.[59]

The IMF concludes that there is a discrepancy between wages and employee contribution in Europe: "In relation to the added production value—which in a way hints at some level of profitability and productivity—European automotive workers do lag behind, if one compares the wage costs with the auto workers wage share worldwide." The discrepancy, according to IMF calculations, is 12 percent and "it is by this amount that European wages should rise so that European wages will correspond to the average wage/productivity level worldwide."[60]

The basis for the IMF approach to Ford is that the output of the individual worker must be related to the total contribution within the company, that is, exports and market share. Furthermore, a company must be treated globally, particularly if it has highly integrated production. National bargaining (and productivity) is a means not only of tactically negating the interest of the worker but also failing to assess his total contribution. Discrepancies on national/subsidiary profit and loss statements reflect national policy (taxation) and corporate policy (internal transfer pricing). Management confuses the issue according to the IMF. Thus it has been in Ford's interest to demonstrate national "losses," such as in the United Kingdom, not only as an antiunion device but also (as in the United Kingdom) to obtain government "bailouts."

The argument that the IMF uses at Ford-Europe, that is, transnational data are relevent, will be used at the ten world councils in the auto industry, according to Casserini.* Casserini told me of a number of specific transnational labor actions undertaken by IMF. They include:

1. Ford-U.K. and Germany shop stewards met to discuss their "mutual interests" during the Ford-U.K. strike in 1971. Although "no romantic ideas" were discussed, they increased cooperation because they build similar models. They have pledged not to do overtime if work has shifted to another plant in their countries.
2. Canadian workers are the most prone to sympathy action, particularly with U.S. and U.K. workers, according to an IMF survey.
3. The Ford Plant in Broadmeadows, Australia, struck in 1971. The IMF affiliate at Ford in Venezuela indicated it wanted to go on a sympathy strike. The Australian workers advised the affiliate not to do it because they were too close to a settlement.
4. Peugeot workers in France called a "spontaneous" half-day sympathy strike with Peugeot workers in Argentina in 1968.
5. Although some ITSs (such as FIET and the ICF) have called for common expiration dates, there has been much IMF opposition to this. It is difficult enough to obtain common expiration dates within a country, particularly England and Germany. Furthermore, if unions were to strike together, there would be too much of a burden upon strike funds. Indeed, many of them would be wiped out.
6. The IMF serves as a conduit for financial assistance to third-world unions and to a "recognition fund" in Spain.
7. An IMF affiliate in Turkey struck the largest foundry there. This was a target case for the union, a significant test of strength. The union appealed to the IMF for assistance. Money was sent through a state bank, but it never arrived. Casserini believes this was due to state interference. The IMF protested to the ILO about "banking practices" and the money arrived. IMF personnel went to Turkey to offer assistance. They were threatened and picketing was forbidden. Their efforts met with little success.
8. English and German affiliates of the IMF have consulted with FIAT, the auto manufacturer, about social development in southern Italy and work methods in that company.
9. The IMF analysis of Ford previously discussed is viewed as a means of increasing "coordinated international bargaining." The IMF opposes transnational collective bargaining because it is not seen as practical. However, if the European company law passes by which multinationals will incorporate Europeanwide, it may occur. The IMF views the ICF's position for transnational collective

---

*Interview with Karl Casserini, assistant general secretary, Social and Economic Department, IMF, Geneva, Switzerland, February 1975.

bargaining as being "utopian." However, through *coordinated* collective bargaining, the IMF will bring forth "public accountability." At future negotiating sessions, detailed information on the following will be brought forth: (a) composition of principal shareholders, minority participation, links with other companies, and so on; (b) geographic location of all plants, indications of production, subcontracting parts and employment figures; and (c) necessary elements for a clear judgment on capital foundation, profitability, and ability to pay, as well as indicators of capital movement.

Dan Benedict, president of the IMF, recently indicated that the detailed strategy previously outlined was only third in a series of phases designed to internationalize labor relations at MNCs. He said that some companies are highly aware of this such as General Electric where "flying joint (GE and IMF) seminars in Latin America were given to workers to induce a wider sense of what they are part of."[61] The IMF clearly is the leading organizational proponent of multinational bargaining.

## INTERNATIONAL CHEMICAL WORKERS FEDERATION

The ICF has been at the center of the most controversy in the international trade union movement. Most of it is a result of statements issued by its president, Charles "Chip" Levinson. To some extent, the data in Chapter 3 bear out some of Levinson's claims, that is, that the ICF has been involved in numerous specific transnational trade union "actions" against the MNC. However, these specific ICF findings are only coincidental to the research and by no means was there an effort to deny or affirm Levinson's claims. Levinson's claims are documented in his *International Trade Unionism* and to some extent in a *Wall Street Journal* interview.[62] As many examples of international trade union activity involve the ICF, it is appropriate to examine them at this point. But one has to note that these data are based only on union claims. They tend to be discussed, overblown, and exaggerated.

### Akzo, 1972

Akzo, a Dutch chemical-textile's multinational firm, determined in 1972 that "measures for a greater concentration [of manufacturing facilities] are of vital importance to the Group's [Akzo's] survival."[63] Plans were made to close plants in the Netherlands, Belgium, and Switzerland, affecting approximately 6,000 employees. As reported by H. Northrup and R. Rowan, the works councils and unions brought pressure upon the Netherlands government, the EEC, and other bodies to save jobs. Subsequently, a "committee of outside experts" was appointed by the Dutch government, the Dutch trade unions, and the Central Employees Works Council of Enka, the Netherlands, to "restructure the company." The report recommended that instead of closing plants, it would be better to cut some production facilities.

During the period when the report was being studied by Akzo management, Dutch, German, and Belgian employees held sit-ins at the Bredar, Netherlands, plant for one week. "As a result, Akzo abandoned its plans to close plants except for the already shut facility in Switzerland where the EEC bureaucracy is not a factor."[64]

There is much dispute about the role of the ICF at Akzo, and other successful transnationally coordinated labor actions. Northrup and Rowan minimize Levinson's role, stating that Akzo "met twice with multinational union delegates, once with a Dutch and German group, and once with a Dutch, German and Belgian group. These delegations were not formed by the ICF or by other interested bodies, but resulted from communications among the unions affected by the proposed closings."[65] Barnet and Muller state, "When Akzo, N.V., announced plans to close three plants in the Netherlands, Belgium and Germany, unions in those countries coordinated strikes which forced the company to abandon its plans. Dutch workers actually occupied the Akzo plant at Bredar. The unions were also able to get the EEC industries Commission to intervene against this proposed massive capital transfer."[66] Although the occupation itself did occur, Northrup and Rowan do not think the ICF had much to do with it.

Whether or not the ICF had a major role in changing Akzo's plan there is agreement that transnational labor coordination was responsible for the shift. The recognition by the Dutch, German, and Belgian trade unionists (most of them affiliated in some way with the ICF) that it was in their interest to coordinate—in much the same manner as a multinational management—indicates that at minimum within the EEC regional cooperation was a necessity. Furthermore, the fact that a non-EEC member, Switzerland, was directly affected, and its unions chose not to respond, is indicative of the weaker regional ties in that country and weaker unions.

### St. Gobain, 1969

The ICF's action against the French-based multinational St. Gobain is the most publicized transnational labor action to date. Affiliates of the ICF in Europe and the United States (glass and ceramics workers at Corning Glass Works) agreed to coordinate all collective bargaining through a special committee designated by the ICF. "The essential point of this agreement was that the unions in each country agreed not to settle their claims with local management before all others were ready to do the same. This was to make sure that the company could not make up the production it might lose through a strike in one country by increasing production in another."[67] This was a major step in the development of coordinated collective bargaining because trade unions were able to develop prior to negotiations a general strategy of support by building negotiating "floors" in one country to be used in another.

> The ICF was able to establish a standing committee with St. Gobain representatives from France, Italy, Germany, the U.S., Belgium, Norway, Sweden and Switzerland. Agreement was reached, "1) to coordinate negotiations in France, Germany, Italy and the U.S.: 2) that no negotiations should be concluded in any country without the approval of the standing committee; 3) that in the event of a strike in one country all unions would provide financial assistance if needed; 4) that if the strike was prolonged, overtime would be stopped at other St. Gobain plants; and 5) that if the company tried to move production from one country to another in order to break or weaken a strike, the move would be resisted."[68]

Although negotiations in each country did not seek the same contract, common objectives were met—except in France where the CGT did not support the agreement.

The importance of the St. Gobain agreement is that it represents the first successful transnational labor coordination of a significant scale. Although there was no necessity to test the plan that the union put forward, there is little doubt that this demonstration of international labor unity pushed St. Gobain to capitulation. A similar claim can be made for the Akzo action; however, the unions involved were reacting to a multinational plant closure as opposed to preparing for a long-range strategy such as St. Gobain. Although coordination was less extensive at Akzo, it did indicate that combined action within the economically integrated area—the EEC—could have a positive result for the unions.

## INTERNATIONAL FEDERATION OF MUSICIANS AND INTERNATIONAL SECRETARIAT OF ENTERTAINMENT TRADE UNIONS

Reference is rarely made to the International Federation of Musicians (IFM) as an international trade secretariat. Indeed, Willatt's report on multinational unions[69] does not include it as one of the 16 ITSs in its "complete" listing. Although the IFM has not been actively engaged on the multinational question, it has developed a program of transnational work rules, perhaps the most extensive of any ITS.

As most of the companies in European broadcasting are state owned, they are multinational by their very nature, as their "products" penetrate national boundaries. Rules have been established "to initiate negotiations with international employer's organizations with a view to agreeing on certain principles that would make it possible by stages to develop a uniform pattern of employment conditions in broadcasting and in the film and the record industries."[70]

Although most of the recorded activity of the IFM in the area of international contracts has been less than substantive, there have been instances of direct transnational ITS assistance. Thus the IFM was requested by the Swiss Musicians Union to approach the American Federation of Musicians concerning noncompliance "with rates of pay on the part of an American orchestra on tour in Switzerland."[71] Similar approaches have been made to record companies when recording in a host country. There have been expressions of solidarity across national boundaries by all affiliates concerning a musicians' strike in Iceland (1966), the Composers Guild strike in the United States, and so on.

Although these instances may seem minor when compared with ICF activity, they do indicate the transnational labor activity of a professional group based upon the promulgation and acceptance of international standards by that group. The IFM has not successfully countered an MNC, for example, RCA; however, through the nature of its organization and profession, it is conceptually a strategic possibility.

Another ITS, the International Secretariat of Entertainment Workers Trades Union (ISETU) "sent information" to the IFM "expressing the wish for better coordination in dealing with occupational problems at international levels, to constitute a common front."[72] The possibility of greater coordination and even merger between ISETU and IFM increases the strategic possibility previously mentioned. ISETU's major contribution is the "progress made in the direction of free movement of entertainment workers between the different member countries. An agreement has been reached between the Belgian entertainment trade union and the German international variety artists union by which the trade union rights and status of workers from each country are protected while in the other."[73]

## AFL-CIO: SUMMARY

The Europeans have been the primary movers behind transnational labor relations as a positive force because many subscribe to a "liberal" view of the MNCs. The U.S. labor movement has been more critical in its formal positions. This is both an expression of its traditional "business" or "antagonistic" relationship with management and its fear of loss of jobs through export. The United States being a headquarters country has, in the AFL-CIO view, lost jobs to overseas markets. Its primary argument is to regulate MNCs through the tax laws.[74]

In early 1976 the AFL-CIO prepared a statement to the Senate Finance Committee concerning foreign income provisions of a tax reform bill indicating support of tax disincentives for foreign investment.[75] This argument, the AFL-CIO notes with pride, is supported by William Frank of Cornell University, who indicates that over 1 million jobs have been lost between 1966 and 1973. Frank stated, "If U.S. MNC's had attempted to serve foreign markets from American production sites instead of from their foreign subsidiaries,"[76] these jobs would have been in the United States. Perhaps the AFL's most convincing argument is that:

> Other major industrial nations regulate the operations of their MNC's through government policies . . . thus restraining their opportunities to move abroad.
>
> The Japanese government, the AFL-CIO says, closely screens foreign investments to assure that foreign operations support maximum growth of the domestic economy. In France foreign exchange regulations, in coordination with national planning, have the effect of regulating the outflow of investment capital. In Sweden companies must get approval from the central bank before they can invest overseas. Every project must be reviewed with particular attention paid to the project's effect on Swedish exports. The United Kingdom closely supervises international capital flows. "National economic planning limits firms' freedom to invest contrary to the national interest—especially when government directly owns a share of major industries."[77]

Although the AFL-CIO has supported efforts by the OECD to obtain a code of conduct on MNCs, its position has frequently been at odds with that of other developed nations. This is because European countries have been the primary recipient of U.S. exported jobs. George Meany, president of the AFL-CIO, has supported the conservative OECD Code, although the AFL has downplayed alternative codes, such as those coming from the ILO. The ILO has a majority representation of developing countries. These efforts to "politicize" this organization, in Meany's view, has reduced the ILO's "technical competence."

The prevailing theme at the ILO's World Employment Conference held in Geneva, Switzerland, in June 1976, is "reflected in background papers ... that MNC's bleed the poorest countries and aggravate their economic woes." However, journalist A. H. Raskin of the *New York Times*, who is frequently considered to be the dean of labor journalists, notes "no such simplistic themes emerged from the informal colloquy among spokesmen for unions representing factory workers in Pakistan, the Philippines, France, Japan and the United States. On the contrary, at least as much was said in praise of multinationals as was said in condemnation. The consensus was that, for the most part, corporations operating across national lines tended to be responsible in their approach to wages and other aspects of industrial relations."[78]

The "simplistic" (Raskin's term) and "political" (Meany's) statements stemming from the ILO have been the reason why Meany pressured the U.S. government to withhold funds from that organization. On June 3, 1976, President Gerald Ford allowed funds to be sent after four years' blockage.

Leonard Woodcock's United Autoworkers has acted quite independently of the AFL-CIO by being the primary U.S. proponent of international activity. Woodcock has called for a modified form of "Germany-style" codetermination at Chrysler,[79] and Pat Greathouse, vice president of the UAW, indicated that "all the countries in which the Big Three in the American farm equipment industry—Deere & Co., International Harvester and Caterpillar—had affiliates to sit in on the opening of contract negotiations in the U.S. three years ago."[80] The UAW, through its International Department, has engaged in other international activities, including participation at the IMF World Auto Councils. It has been the primary U.S. trade union force on the multinational issue.

Other trade unions, including the Teamsters, the Office and Professional Employees International Union, and the International Association of Machinists, have also participated at world conferences. Most AFL-CIO affiliated unions, however, have been hindered by Meany's position.

## TRADE UNIONS AND THE MNCs: PRESENT STATUS

Within the past two years, the OECD, the ILO, the "group of eminent persons" designated by the UN, and the European Parliament have addressed the impact of MNCs on working people. The MNC has in effect been recognized as a political entity capable of exercising "power" and "influence," in Lasswellian terms, and "authoritatively allocating values," on the Eastonian model. Trade unions and their international organizations have been the primary countervailing force to express concerns about MNCs through government organizations.

On June 21, 1976, the OECD ratified the multinational code of conduct. To a great extent, the code is the product of a compromise between the international business community and international organized labor. MNCs will be expected to demonstrate how they will "voluntarily comply" with the code and the Badger case involving a subsidiary of Raytheon is a good example. The issue involved the payment of severance to Belgian workers. The unions argued that in spite of corporate considerations the company is bound to pay severance to comply with the spirit of the OLCD code. Raytheon to date disagrees, claiming that they are legally protected from not paying. Another impact will be for MNCs to disclose finances on a "geographic area basis."[81] This will permit trade unions to obtain financial data beyond their national borders. As noted previously, the IMF, Postal Telegraphic Trade Secretariat, FIET, and other trade unions have consistently called for financial disclosure beyond the borders of the host country. The OECD Code, although voluntary, is the first manifestation of a "victory" on this issue.

The European Parliament has accepted draft proposals under which businesses operating in the EEC would register to become "European companies." Financial disclosure would be EEC-wide and transnational standards for mergers and accounting practices would emerge. As has been noted, international trade secretariats have called for the end of transfer pricing. Although the European draft proposals do not specifically address this issue, European union lobbyists believe the statute will be the "first step" toward this. The statute will also have "worker-directors" on a Europewide basis. Although representation proportions have not been developed, there will be a supervisory board responsible for broad policies, including investments transnationally throughout the EEC.

The Committee on Transnational Corporations was established by the UN "group of eminent persons." It is its mandate to establish a code of conduct on MNCs. Nat Weinberg, former vice president and economist of the UAW, is the labor representative to the group, and he has indicated that vigorous efforts will be made for a forceful official position on MNCs.[82]

Weinberg told the International Industrial Relations Conference in Montreal that the code being developed by the Committee on Transnational Corporations is similar to the official position of the ICFTU.* This includes (1) Governments should adopt "liberal" practices on sympathy strikes. This would call for the repeal of sections of the U.S. Taft-Hartley Act. (2) International accounting standards should be adopted

---

*See the section on the ICFTU for details.

for "special reliance" in collective bargaining. (3) MNCs should act as "spearheads" for good labor practices. (4) Emphasis should be placed on home-country controls rather than host because home countries are usually stronger bargainers.[83]

The trade union movement is well aware of the desire of MNCs to keep the international movement at no more than the "exchange of information" level. It has approached the issue tactically as if it were going into a collective bargaining session. A senior TUAC official stated to the OECD, "Indeed the trade union position taken in November, 1975, was kept *deliberately low key* in order to ensure that an early agreement could be reached on a limited number of issues considered by the trade union structure of November as the *minimum* at this stage." The official indicates that trade unions actually desire " 'country by country' disclosure of information," and "negotiations at the appropriate level of management authority" with *appropriate* level defined as "including the *headquarters* of the multinational enterprise."

Major multinational codes have been in effect since mid-1977. The extent of their force of implementation varies; however, they will all have the moral force of either their government or the UN behind them. U.S. MNCs have already been told that their government expects a high level of compliance with the OECD code, as the United States was a principal architect and business opinions were elicited prior to passage by their primary representative group, the U.S. Chamber of Commerce.[84] The ILO Code will have less credibility because of the AFL-CIO's position. The Committee on Transnational Corporations has the potential of offering an acceptable code because of the nature of its supporters (the "group of eminent persons") and active U.S. participation in its development.

Each of the international trade secretariats previously described, as well as other trade union bodies—including those of the United Kingdom and Scandinavia—have actively pursued a policy of international coordination. To some extent, their efforts are coming to fruition through the codes. More concrete efforts have already resulted, for example, Akzo and St. Gobain.

To summarize, the public record of European trade unions indicates a significant trend toward dealing with MNCs on a transnational basis. The attacks are so specific against the MNC that one cannot escape the conclusion that the MNC has been a motivating force for this Europeanwide effort. Workers are perceiving that it is in their interest to join with workers in other countries to increase their leverage against MNCs. This is reflected in both the national and international position papers of trade union bodies. The full extent of their efforts, including those without "formal" positions (most of the French unions), has never been explored. This will be done in Chapter 3.

## NOTES

1. R. J. Barnet and R. E. Muller, *Global Reach—The Power of the Multinational Corporations* (New York: Simon & Schuster, 1974).

2. Postal, Telegraph and Telephone International, Seventh Asian Regional Conference, Melbourne, Australia, September 16–20, 1974, Item 8 of the Agenda: Special Study Report on Multinational Companies.

3. World Confederation of Labor (WCL), "For a Policy to Cope with Multinational Companies," extracts from the World Confederation of Labor Congress, September 1973, p. 4.

4. International Confederation of Free Trade Unions (ICFTU), "The Multinational Challenge," Conference Reports no. 2, Brussels, Belgium, September 1971, p. 15.

5. E. Roberts, *Workers Control* (London: Allen & Unwin, 1973), p. 122.

6. ICFTU, *The Multinational Challenge*, p. 22.

7. Postal, Telegraph and Telephone International, Seventh Asian Regional Conference, p. 21.

8. The AFL-CIO has produced a study indicating that MNCs were responsible for a net loss of 500,000 jobs between 1966 and 1969 in the United States. *New York Times*, December 22, 1974, sec. 4, p. 3.

9. Roberts, *Workers Control*, p. 8.

10. Howard V. Perlmutter, "Towards Research on and Development of Nations, Unions and Firms as World-wide Institutions," in *Transnational Industrial Relations. The Impact of Multinational Corporations and Economic Regionalism to Industrial Relations*, ed. Hans Gunter (New York: Macmillan/St. Martin's Press, 1972), p. 44.

11. Charles Levinson, *Industry's Democratic Revolution* (London: Allen & Unwin, 1974), pp. 25–56.

12. *Council of Nordic Trade Unions (NFS) Confronting the Multinational Companies: Action Programme,* Stockholm, January 1975, p. 5.

13. Ibid., p. 6.

14. Ibid., p. 10.

15. *Industrial Democracy,* report by the TUC General Council to the 1974 Trade Union Congress, London, England.

16. Trades Union Congress, *International Companies*, Congress House, London, October 21, 1970, p. 3.

17. Ibid.

18. Ibid., p. 4.

19. Ibid., p. 33.

20. G. S. Viner, National Union of Journalists, as quoted in Trades Union Congress *Report of a Conference on International Companies,* (London: Congress House, October 21, 1970) p. 39.

21. Ibid.

22. Clive Jenkins, ibid., p. 41.

23. See *Industrial Relations Europe* 4, no. 38 (January 1976): As part of the Chrysler "rescue plan," 6,000 workers were to be laid off immediately. Some of the production of a new car originally scheduled for France would be shifted to England. The communist

Confédéracion Général du Travail (CGT) union in France "promises trouble for Chrysler's French subsidiary" if the shift goes through. *Business Europe* 16, no. 2 (January 9, 1976): 10.

24. Jenkins, Trade Union Congress, *International Companies*.

25. *Industrial Democracy*, p. 40.

26. Norris Willatt, *Multinational Unions* (London: Financial Times, 1974), p. 7.

27. ICFTU, "The Multinational Challenge," p. 19.

28. Ibid., p. 31.

29. Ibid., p. 11.

30. *Business Europe*, December 12, 1975, p. 394.

31. *Financial Times*, September 1975, p. 10.

32. Willatt, *Multinational Unions*, p. 13.

33. WCL, "For a Policy to Cope with Multinational Companies," p. 4.

34. Ibid., p. 9.

35. Ibid.

36. Wright interview.

37. WCL, "For a Policy to Cope with Multinational Companies."

38. International Federation of Commercial, Clerical and Technical Employees, Facing Multinationals—The Strategy of FIET, internal, confidential document, Geneva, Switzerland, 1973, 17 OC/11/6, p. 2.

39. Ibid., p. 3.

40. Ibid.

41. Ibid., p. 4.

42. Ibid.

43. Ibid., p. 5.

44. Ibid., p. 6.

45. Ibid., p. 8.

46. Duane Kujawa, *International Labor Relations Management in the Automobile Industry* (New York: Praeger, 1971).

47. Interview with Nat Weinberg, United Nations, New York, June 1975.

48. Everett M. Kassalow, "The International Metalworkers Federation and the Multinational Automobile Companies," unpublished manuscript, University of Wisconsin, Madison, March 1974.

49. Ibid., p. 8.

50. Ibid., p. 9.

51. Ibid., p. 12.

52. Ibid.

53. Ibid., p. 28.

54. "IMF Systematic Analysis of Multinational Companies Worldwide and at Subsidiary Level, I. The Ford Motor Company," Geneva, Switzerland, October 1974, p. 3.

55. Ibid.

56. Ibid.

57. Ibid., p. 5.

58. Ibid., p. 2.

59. Ibid.

60. Ibid., p. 6.

61. Dan Benedict, president, IMF, speech made at International Conference on Trends in Industrial and Labor Relations, Workshop on Union Reaction to Multinational Corporations, Montreal, May 27, 1976.

62. Richard Janssen, *Wall Street Journal*, June 17, 1974, p. 1.

63. H. Northrup and R. Rowan, "Multinational Collective Bargaining Activity: The Factual Record in Chemicals, Glass, and Rubber Tires. Pt. II," *Columbia Journal of World Business* (Summer 1974): 49–62.

64. Ibid., p. 51.

65. Ibid., p. 52.

66. Barnet and Muller, *Global Reach*, p. 314.

67. Eric Jacobs, *European Trade Unionism* (New York: Holmes and Meier, 1973).

68. Christopher Tugendhat, *The Multinationals* (Middlesex, England: Penguin Books, 1973), p. 226.

69. Willatt, *Multinational Unions*.

70. International Federation of Musicians; "Report on the Activity," Seventh Business Period, Autumn 1969-Autumn 1972, London, p. 23.

71. Ibid., p. 28.

72. Willatt, *Multinational Unions*, p. 91.

73. Ibid.

74. U. S., Congress, Senate, Committee on Finance, *Multinational Corporations: A Compendium of Papers Submitted to the Subcommittee*, 93rd Congress, 1st sess., 1973.

75. Confidential report in *Washington International Intelligence Bulletin*, a service of International Business Government Counsellors, Washington, D.C., June 4, 1976.

76. Ibid., p. 2.

77. Ibid., p. 3.

78. A. H. Raskin, *New York Times*, June 4, 1976, p. D7.

79. Leonard Woodcock, cited in *New York Times*, 1976.

80. *Washington International Intelligence Bulletin*.

81. Draft, "Declaration of OECD Member Governments on International Investment and Multinational Enterprises," May 20, 1976, p. Annex-5.

82. Nat Weinberg, former vice president, UAW, speech made at International Conference on Trends in Industrial and Labor Relations, Workshop on Internationalization of Industrial Relations—The Growth of Multinational Corporations and Unions—Response of International Organizations, Montreal, May 26, 1976. See the section on the ICFTU for details.

83. Weinberg speech, Montreal, 1976.

84. International Chamber of Commerce, business briefing on the OECD Code, Washington, D.C., June 1, 1976.

# 3 INTERNATIONAL LABOR TRANSACTIONS

## THE BASIS OF INTERACTION

Having looked at the efforts of trade unions to gain leverage against the MNCs, we shall now turn briefly to the implications of this for political science, specifically political integration. We have already noted that the empirical data utilized are essentially transaction data, a tool of the communications school. If we go beyond this and view international labor transactions in the broader context of theory, we find some interesting observations.

As a step toward seeing the broader context, we can look to Joseph Nye's perception of integration as process. Nye examines the transactions created by regional economic groupings of interest groups and views a high level of these transactions as a necessary condition for political integration. Thus, by examining a specific interest group, EEC or Scandinavia, we have a departure point for examining the empirical data in this chapter. Furthermore, the material concerns of the communications theorists, systems analysts, and neofunctionalists with the importance of welfare goals, the influence of mass community, and the rates of interaction among actors indicate that labor-management relations may be an ideal test to determine the extent of political integration as measured by the international transactions in that interest group.

Trade unions have created the basis for a web of international transactions through the development of a network of regional organizations. These organizations are an outgrowth of the trend reflecting industrial centralization within each European nation.

National trade union organizations exist in each European country. Typically they are organized by industry and affiliate with a national center. Organizational complexity increases at the international level because there is a direct reflection of political, industrial, and, to some extent, religious differences. Thus there is a potential for a high number (and to some extent, duplication) of communications (or transactions) across national boundaries. To demonstrate this, consider the major clerical union in the United Kingdom, ASTMS, which belongs not only to a national center, the Trades Union Congress, but through that to the liberal international center for free world unions, the ICFTU. ASTMS, as a primary organizer of white-collar employees, mainly in the financial industry, also belongs to FIET, the International Clerical Trade Secretariat. Thus ASTMS belongs to three international "communications" centers, each of which, coincidentally, addresses the issue of MNCs.

The transaction ability for a national trade union therefore has few limitations. It may communicate formally either through a national trade union body, such as the AFL-CIO, to the major "political" international federation or to unions in similar industries through an ITS. The measurement of these transactions and their direction, frequency, and intensity should indicate to what extent workers through their representatives, the trade union elite, have developed a transnational movement. By viewing political integration as Nye does, as a process, the extent to which the potential for political integration has occurred can, according to Nye, be determined. The flow of transactions from interest groups such as trade unions will be an indication of this integration potential.

L. Lindberg and S. A. Scheingold have noted that one of the very purposes why groups organize is to maintain contacts and secure information. As seen in Chapter 2, international trade union bodies have developed a high level of information exchange. The bulk of these data has in one form or another concerned the MNC. Such cases as Akzo, St. Gobain, and the development of the TUAC position on the OECD could not have arisen without a sophisticated network for exchanging information among unions across national borders. This occurred, to some extent, regardless of the organizational memberships of a trade union, particularly with respect to TUAC. As Akzo and St. Gobain both have unions affiliated with the same ITS, the International Chemical Workers Federation, the ability to organize against an MNC in one industry was facilitated.

To the extent that an MNC has many unions belonging to the same international trade secretariat, it would appear that trade union interaction across national borders about that company would be common. The questionnaire data will be examined to determine to what extent there has been specific transnational cooperation against the MNC and to some extent particular MNCs.

Lindberg and Scheingold indicate that the concept of political integration is related to the locus of decision making. It is their implication that the determination of where decision making lies is an indication of the level of political integration. Howard Perlmutter and Hans Gunter are also concerned with this relationship. Gunter's box model, which utilizes Perlmutter's concept of categorizing MNCs by their locus of decision making, notes that a geocentric MNC (dispersed locus of decision making) has within it a high "propensity for industrial relations to transnationalize." Thus truly transnational labor relations should be found in those companies that have decentralized decision-making authority based in the host country.

Although the concern with the locus of decision making in specific MNCs is not in the context of this book, one can, to some extent, look at the potential for a central locus of decision making in trade unions. There is a trend toward organizational coalescing in Europe, although it is believed that no national trade union center has given up its decision-making authorities. The WCL and ICFTU have merged within Europe, and there has been an accelerated development of other transnational labor bodies, such as the Nordic Council and the European Metalworkers Federation. One can therefore hypothesize that there is a high level of transnational communication, minimumally at the exchange of information level in Europe. Certainly much of this concerns the MNC as testified by the positions on the MNC examined in Chapter 2.

What level of communication has actively occurred as a result of this organizational coalescing with respect to a broad spectrum of interaction will now be examined. The focus will be on the forms of interaction as well as on their level of intensity. In essence, the question to be answered is: Are Nye and Lindberg and Scheingold correct that regional economic groupings create a flow of transactions having a high potential for political unity, or are the obstacles to transnational labor action too great to overcome the traditional national approach of trade unions? This assertion by Lindberg and Scheingold (and to some extent by Nye) will be tested in the forthcoming data.

There are various forms of trade union interaction. Some of them have already been noted:

1. Organizational coalescing across national borders, particularly in Europe.

2. The exchange of information. This is notable in the U.K. Trades Union Congress, the Nordic Trade Council, and the International Metalworkers Federation.
3. The acceleration of the acceptance of the concept of codetermination in various forms to promote workers' participation in management. This concept originated in Germany and has been proposed in most countries in the EEC. Unions have supported codetermination in lobbying efforts at the EEC level by proposing the "fifth directive," a form of codetermination to be instituted when a European company law is adopted. MNCs would register as "European companies" as opposed to national companies.
4. Ideological organization through the ICFTU, WCL, and WFTU. The major ideological splits (communist, liberal, social democrat, and so on) have been demonstrated on the worker participation issue. Most notably, the French and Italian communist centers, CGT and CGIL, have reflected the Marxist approach to MNCs and are opposed to worker participation on management boards of MNCs.
5. Specific MNC action by unions within the same ITS: Akzo, St. Gobain, and others detailed in Chapter 2.
6. International sympathy action: Peugeot Metalworkers supporting Latin American strikers.
7. Legislative action: the Council of Nordic Trade Unions seeking the right to international strike support at each legislature in Scandinavia.
8. World councils. These have been organized by ITSs against a specific MNC, for example, the IMF World Auto Councils.
9. Pressure for an MNC code. The ILO, OECD, and the UN will all have codes on labor relations as a result of pressure by trade unions.
10. International collective bargaining. Various trade secretariats have made extensive preparation for bargaining.[1]

Communications theorists have postulated that by quantifying these interactions, statements can be made about the level of integration these units (trade unions) have. Although communications theory was primarily concerned with the state as actor, Lindberg and Scheingold and Nye have demonstrated that one should view integration as a process. Interest groups and regional economic groups in particular should be looked at. One can then adapt communications transactions to interest groups, for example, trade unions, and determine the state of the process of political integration this leads us to.

Utilizing the questionnaire, these transactions will be examined, particularly the form in which these transactions occur; whether different forms are used depending on whether activity is national or transnational; how intense this activity is (active or passive); and if there is a significant level of transnational activity directed specifically against the MNC.

## INTERNATIONAL LABOR TRANSACTIONS: EMPIRICAL DATA

### The Forms of Transaction

Trade unions display and achieve their influence in numerous ways. The most familiar in the United States is collective bargaining with a specific company, which may lead to a type of industrial action such as strikes or slowdowns. In continental Europe, collective bargaining primarily occurs on an industrywide basis with supplemental agreements written at the company level. Thus a centralized vehicle for trade union activity exists at the national level to which the U.S.-based MNC has little or no experience in the home country: the industrywide collective agreement. European unions therefore are more organizationally prepared than those in the United States to participate in a coordinated activity.

After reviewing the international trade union literature, I have concluded that interunion coordinating activity either assumes or has the potential for assuming seven major forms:

1. The exchange of information, including data on MNC investments and employee population.
2. Informal consultation of trade union leaders.
3. Scheduled meetings to plan a strategy.
4. Joint collective bargaining, including international coalescing across national borders to engage in international negotiations with MNCs. As one company may have different collective agreements with different unions, the coalescing of these unions to form a single bargaining power is a potential powerful force.
5. Legislative influence. At the national level, trade unions bring their influence to bear through familiar means, including lobbying or through a directly affiliated political party. At the international level, this influence may be more discrete. Included in this form are different national trade unions developing a planned legislative platform or international lobbying at the European Parliament.
6. Strike fund assistance. The sharing of a pool of funds or lending direct financial assistance to workers in another country represents a potent weapon to support international labor action.
7. International sympathy strikes. As at the national level, the strike is labor's ultimate weapon, particularly if it occurs within the same MNC in support of workers in another foreign "branch" of

that company. In some countries, for example, the United Kingdom, these are illegal.

### The Extent of International Labor Transactions

These forms of international labor action are an extension of standard labor tactics utilized at the national level. To test the degree to which they are utilized, a questionnaire was developed and sent to 150 labor bodies, including national centers, international trade secretariats, world federations, and some local unions. As transnational action occurs to varying degrees at all of these levels, and I wanted to test the extent of international coordination, it was thought appropriate to send them to each level of trade union bodies. Even accounting for an exaggeration of union claims, the data have statistical significance based upon an over one-third response—56 unions. Attempts to verify these claims with companies proved difficult because of their reluctance to respond to a questionnaire. Nevertheless, the data should be of high interest.

The questionnaires were sent to European labor bodies as well as a small number of U.S. labor groups, particularly those which are known in the literature either to advocate or have participated in international labor activity. Fifty-six (37 percent) trade union bodies responded. Tables 3.1 to 3.3 specify ideological and worker type characteristics, as well as how each union organizationally is placed in the labor movement.

An effort was also made to determine MNC perception of international trade union activity by sending major MNCs a "management" questionnaire. The intention was to direct essentially the same ques-

**TABLE 3.1**  Type of Union Organization

|  | Absolute Frequency | Relative Frequency (Percent) |
|---|---|---|
| No information | 5 | 8.9 |
| International trade secretariat | 6 | 10.7 |
| Central national trade union | 40 | 71.4 |
| Local union | 5 | 8.9 |
| Total | 56 | 100.0 |
| Valid observations—56 |  | Missing observations—0 |

It should be noted that most union responses were from national unions. This is reflective of the structure of the union movement.

## TABLE 3.2  Ideology and Religion

|  | Absolute Frequency | Relative Frequency (Percent) |
|---|---|---|
| Not known | 18 | 32.1 |
| Catholic | 5 | 8.9 |
| Communist and allies | 1 | 1.8 |
| Left socialist | 2 | 3.6 |
| Social democrat or right socialist | 22 | 39.3 |
| Business | 2 | 3.6 |
| Protestant | 1 | 1.8 |
| Other | 5 | 8.9 |
| Total | 56 | 100.0 |
| Valid observations—56 | | Missing observations—0 |

This distribution of unions is about what should be expected. Most European unions do fall within the social democratic perspective, with increasing radicalization of formerly moderate unions in certain countries, for example, the CFDT in France. The business category is for the only two U.S. union organizations in the survey, the UAW and AFL-CIO. In my judgment, they are further to the right than the social democratic unions in Europe, although one would consider the international policies of the UAW as being social democratic.

The collected data should not be considered significant because there were 18 "not known" observations. This was due to a lack of ability to identify certain unions within the aforementioned categories. The four unions identified as Catholic or Protestant were all in the Netherlands. They either are themselves or belong to religious union federations within the Netherlands. Furthermore, they include such a broad spectrum of thought that it would be inaccurate to identify them closely with a political position.

Only 30 unions were clearly identified with an "ideology." This is not enough representation to determine whether the extent of transnational action against MNCs is related to ideology.

A chart was developed comparing responses within the small samples (not shown). It was found that 100 percent of the communist unions scheduled joint meetings transnationally to plan strategy on MNCs and 53 percent of the social democratic ones also did so. Little significance should be attributed to this because the sample for social democrats was large and for communists small (only one). The level of activity was approximately the same rank as found in Table 3.14. The distribution of "yes" and "no" responses also did not seem related to ideology. However, in order to make statements covering the importance of ideology, one would need a greater level of union response.

tions about union activity to MNCs, compare responses, and determine if the reality of the union response matched the perception of the MNCs. However, and to the extent that could be expected, corporate managements were more circumspect than labor. Only 12 percent replied for a total of 16 companies.

The companies did have a major interest in learning the survey results. Repeated requests were received for disclosure of the completed data by certain companies.

**TABLE 3.3** Worker Type

| | Absolute Frequency | Relative Frequency (Percent) |
|---|---|---|
| Not known | 12 | 21.4 |
| Blue collar | 19 | 33.9 |
| White collar | 8 | 14.3 |
| Professional and supervisor | 12 | 21.4 |
| Blue and white collar | 5 | 8.9 |
| Total | 56 | 100.0 |
| Valid observations—56 | | Missing observations—0 |

Many unions in Europe organize only certain professions—skill level is important. Again, because of small sample size, identifying trends in this category were not pursued.

**Trade Union Responses**

Let us now proceed to review the trade union responses to determine their utilization of the previously described forms of interaction.

Each union was asked if it engages or cooperates with other unions or labor federations concerning each previously described category of interaction. The objective was to find out how extensive transnational labor cooperation is in both a general sense and specifically against MNCs. The questionnaire called for circling "never," "seldom," "frequently," or "confidential." For the purpose of analysis, "never" was counted as "no"; "seldom," "frequently," and "confidential" were "yes." There were very few "confidentials," and it was assumed that a union or company might not wish to go on record by indicating a positive reply, so "confidential" could be a good way out of indicating "yes" without saying so. Furthermore, as the literature points to very few transnational incidents, it was thought that "seldom" should be viewed as an achievement. A union only needs one incident of transnational collective bargaining to establish a precedent for forthcoming negotiations.

To respond to our concerns, the national/international utilization of a transaction form will first be reviewed. Definitions (reference questionnaire): (1) National: at another plant in same geographic area, MNC within the country, within federation in the country, cross-federation within country. (2) International: within MNC between countries, cross-federation between countries.

The percentages in Tables 3.4–3.10 are based upon total respondents replying to a question. If no answer was given ("missing"), that was not considered a response.

Each category response shows over a 25 percent level of those answering to having engaged in an international labor activity. Although each percentage is lower in the international area than national area, considering the obstacles one finds to international union activity, such as legal, organizational, and perceived self-interest of union leaders to act upon immediate and direct (national) needs of their constit-

**TABLE 3.4    Exchange of Information**

| National (Percent) | | | International (Percent) | | |
|---|---|---|---|---|---|
| Yes | No | Missing | Yes | No | Missing |
| 154 (90.5) | 16 (9.5) | 55 | 60 (73.1) | 22 (26.9) | 29 |

As close to three quarters of the unions' trade information cross national boundaries, this would appear to be a common and important practice.

**TABLE 3.5    Irregular Consultation**

| National (Percent) | | | International (Percent) | | |
|---|---|---|---|---|---|
| Yes | No | Missing | Yes | No | Missing |
| 128 (83.1) | 26 (17.9) | 66 | 50 (64.9) | 27 (35.1) | 34 |

Irregular consultation as well as other categories are difficult to define precisely. Generally, it refers to infrequent discussion covering the planning of a labor strategy. One would expect, particularly concerning international consultation, that there would be much less frequency of this occurring than the "exchange of information." Surprisingly, this was not the case. The difference is less than 9 percent at both national and international levels.

**TABLE 3.6    Scheduled Joint Meetings**

| National (Percent) | | | International (Percent) | | |
|---|---|---|---|---|---|
| Yes | No | Missing | Yes | No | Missing |
| 140 (83.3) | 28 (16.7) | 56 | 50 (60.2) | 33 (39.8) | 29 |

The difference between the national and international utilization of the two previous forms of transaction averaged 17.8 percent. As scheduled joint meetings is the first of our truly active forms of trade union activity, one would expect a larger gap between national and international categories. This is because of the aforementioned obstacles to interactive activity, including language, the national-based tradition of trade unions, and lack of finances. Thus it is not surprising to find a 23.1 percent difference favoring national activity in this category.

**TABLE 3.7** Joint Collective Bargaining

| National (Percent) | | | International (Percent) | | |
|---|---|---|---|---|---|
| Yes | No | Missing | Yes | No | Missing |
| 112 | 51 | 59 | 21 | 54 | 36 |
| (68.7) | (31.3) | | (28.0) | (72.0) | |

This is the most controversial area of international labor relations. The question of a definition of collective bargaining is at the core of the discussion. For management, it may mean an agreed-upon contract; for labor, merely the discussion of a contract without reaching an agreement constitutes collective bargaining. Each side wishes to claim a "history." By saying they have or have not engaged in collective bargaining as a process establishes a precedent for future agreements. Thus labor is quick to say it engaged in such activity by having management "recognize" non-national labor bodies through mere discussion at the table. Management refuses to label this "bargaining."

For the purpose of analysis we will accept the unions' view—they were the respondents—with full realization that they may have been too generous in their definitions of collective bargaining. Nevertheless, a 28 percent "yes" response is extremely impressive. Prior to this, observers, particularly those of the minor impact school, would say that no such activity occurred. It is also interesting that this category has the widest gap between national and international (40.7 percent), which particularly validates our original expectations, that is, that joint collective bargaining is far less prevalent at the international level.

**TABLE 3.8** Attempt to Influence a Legislative Body

| National (Percent) | | | International (Percent) | | |
|---|---|---|---|---|---|
| Yes | No | Missing | Yes | No | Missing |
| 117 | 49 | 56 | 38 | 42 | 31 |
| (40.4) | (29.6) | | (47.5) | (52.5) | |

Although legislative efforts were higher at the international level than national, I find this category too vague. This often refers to the European Parliament or attempts to influence national legislature. For example, the IMF may lobby, either through headquarters or a German affiliate, before the French legislature—perhaps even covertly. I did not find any hard data or explanation to support this, although efforts to establish a European company law have been vigorously attempted by the ITSs. Generally, I discount this category as a significant finding.

uents, it is surprising that these percentages are so high. (Again note the caveat about union claims.)

Table 3.11 depicts this information more graphically. Each category in the table has been classified as active or passive. The basic criterion for classifying one category as active would be: Have specific visible results been generated? Thus a scheduled joint meeting, joint collective bargaining, financial assistance, and strike funds are all tangible evidence of union activity. Scheduled meetings, although of a

**TABLE 3.9** Strike Fund Assistance

| National (Percent) | | | International (Percent) | | |
|---|---|---|---|---|---|
| Yes | No | Missing | Yes | No | Missing |
| 93 | 63 | 65 | 36 | 39 | 37 |
| (59.6) | (40.4) | | (48.0) | (52.0) | |

The high level of international strike fund support is extremely important for the future of transnational labor activity. The financial commitment by unions outside their borders indicates that they are serious about this activity.

**TABLE 3.10** Sympathy Strike

| National (Percent) | | | International (Percent) | | |
|---|---|---|---|---|---|
| Yes | No | Missing | Yes | No | Missing |
| 94 | 65 | 65 | 31 | 44 | 37 |
| (59.1) | (40.9) | | (41.3) | (58.7) | |

International sympathy strikes are an effective means of transnational support. It is frequently mentioned in the literature as a potent weapon that such strikes are hindered by national law in some countries. It may at times be the first stage of a process leading to transnational collective bargaining.

lower order of activity than joint collective bargaining, are a relatively new step for trade union coordination. The world councils were not formed until the late 1960s. These meetings and others therefore should be considered significant activity.

Coordinated labor activity at the national level is well developed with over 50 percent "yes" to all questions. The more than 50 percent positive response to three of the eight categories within international activity indicates that transnational labor activity is indeed a reality. Although the highest percentage for coordination occurs at the information exchange level, active international coordination occurs with respect to holding consultations and scheduling meetings. This appears to confirm Northrup and Rowan's research that "such consultation, which is consistent with European traditions, may well continue, but negotiations and collective bargaining agreements do not appear to be likely in the foreseeable future."[2]

International tactics appear to be developing in a different order than those utilized nationally. Although information exchange is of primary importance in both arenas, all others are different in the rankings. The major difference is with respect to joint collective bargaining across national borders. My interpretation of the high response level to

TABLE 3.11    Scale of Activity

| | National | | Passive or Active | International | |
|---|---|---|---|---|---|
| | Percent-age | Rank | | Percent-age | Rank |
| Exchange of information | 90.5 | 1 | P | 73.0 | 1 |
| Scheduled joint meetings | 83.3 | 2 | A | 60.2 | 3 |
| Irregular consultation | 83.1 | 3 | P | 64.0 | 2 |
| Attempt to influence a legislative body | 70.4 | 4 | P | 47.5 | 5 |
| Joint collective bargaining | 68.7 | 5 | A | 28.0 | 7 |
| Strike fund assistance | 59.6 | 6 | A | 48.0 | 4 |
| Sympathy strike | 59.1 | 7 | A | 41.3 | 6 |

joint collective bargaining is that different definitions of this were held by some respondents. Daniel Benedict of the International Metalworkers Federation indicated in his questionnaire response that "in two or three cases, joint meetings have been taken up on one or more items that might fall within the area of collective bargaining—but not as part of any broad 'collective agreements.'"*

Many of the union respondents either qualified or gave additional information about their answers. The Confederation of Salaried Employees in Finland (TUK) confirmed some of the general information given in Chapter 2 about the Nordic Council. It indicated that there was frequent collective action undertaken transnationally by these unions except in the one area that is now outlawed—sympathy strikes. It was specifically mentioned that there is "also financial assistance from joint strike funds," and that TUK has engaged in consumer boycotts against South Africa. TUK also engaged in sympathy action to support Chilean workers.

The Northern Carpet Trade Union in the United Kingdom indicated that it exchanged statistical data through the International Textile Garment and Leather Workers and had engaged in information picketing to support the Farah strike in Texas. As a matter of policy it will support the "international trade union movement through the

---

*Daniel Benedict, president, IMF, questionnaire response (code no. 216).

British TUC." When reviewing the International Textile Federation's questionnaire—and I assume it was completed independently of its U.K. member union (this ITS is based in Geneva)—there is confirmation of these points.

The International Textile Workers said that, in addition to support of the Farah strike, it has supported policy changes in South Africa and Holland and has used bargaining gains in one country as leverage in Germany, Holland, France, and the United Kingdom. Furthermore, it sent international representatives to offer bargaining assistance between countries.

The World Federation of Workers in the Food, Tobacco and Hotel Industries said that transnational bargaining had occurred over wages in Holland and Belgium in the tobacco industry. It had used settlements in one country as leverage in the other (between these two countries).

The French professional and supervisory (cadres) union for the chemical and pharmaceutical industries indicated that it had engaged in international wage negotiations without stating where this had occurred. Indeed, by indicating "confidential" to "refusal to work overtime in support of a work stoppage in the same MNC," it is possible that it may have participated in a transnational MNC labor action. The ICF claims in this area are well known and detailed in Chapter 2. The French Cadres Union appears to be confirming these claims—an implicit support of Levinson's contentions.

The Danish Labor Federation (LO) clarified its questionnaire responses by indicating that it had undertaken strike action in support of workers in the United Kingdom. The Danish Metalworkers confirmed the extent of its federation's transnational activity by pointing to specific strikes it had organized in Denmark to support KLM employees in the United States. Furthermore, the Danish Metalworkers indicated that there was an agreement among metalworkers in Scandinavia, including Finland, to share strike funds.

The German Employees Union (DAG), a federation for salaried workers, stated in its questionnaire "In general, it is to state, that we do work on the national level. We do have, of course, contacts with unions in other countries and also continents. Furthermore, *we have a really frequent exchange of information and opinions on the international level.*"*

---

*Letter from Harry Ortmann, international director, DAG, October 9, 1974 (emphasis added).

## Trade Unions and MNCs

Is the MNC a motivating force for transnational action as tested by the present reality of such action directed against MNCs? The data in Table 3.12 indicate specific responses by unions of activity against MNCs. It is a focal point for both national and international activity.

The reason why percentages have been taken excluding the "missing" answers is that some of those "missing" may have not engaged in a specific tactic or would prefer not to so disclose. A "confidential" reply, however, was counted as a "yes" because if so indicated, the probability was high that it had engaged in that tactic.

**TABLE 3.12** Union-MNC Activity Level

| | Active or Passive | MNC Within Country (National Coordination) | | Within MNC Between Countries (International Coordination) | |
|---|---|---|---|---|---|
| | | Percentage | Rank | Percentage | Rank |
| Exchange of information | P | 83.7 | 1 | 75.6 | 1 |
| Scheduled joint meetings | A | 75.6 | 2 | 61.0 | 3 |
| Irregular consultation | P | 69.2 | 3 | 64.9 | 2 |
| Attempt to influence a legislative body | P | 67.5 | 4 | 43.6 | 4 |
| Joint collective bargaining | A | 65.0 | 5 | 31.6 | 7 |
| Sympathy strike | A | 57.9 | 6 | 37.8 | 6 |
| Strike fund assistance | A | 54.3 | 7 | 41.7 | 5 |

*Summary**

| National: MNC (Percent) | | International: MNC (Percent) | |
|---|---|---|---|
| Active | Passive | Active | Passive |
| 38.8 | 63.8 | 43.6 | 29.4 |

*Percentages are of the total number of "yes" responses in each category divided by the total number of respondents, excluding the "missing."

Passive activity vis-a-vis the MNC is most preponderant at the national level, as indicated in Table 3.11. It is noteworthy that internationally active activity is higher than passive (the reverse is true nationally), although the gap between the two classifications is closer internationally than for national responses. The meaning of this is important. The international strategy of the trade unions, when looking at the totality of their tactics, places greater effort within their international strategy on active measures. The MNC by its very nature calls for an international strategy of action by trade unions. At the national level, passive activity predominates at the present time. Thus it could be argued that either the gains to be made have been made to assume leverage on the MNC or that an international strategy is more appropriate to harness the MNC. I expect that both of these are true, but it must also be realized that international objectives, such as coordinating international strikes and engaging in transnational bargaining against a single company, require more "action" because of the relatively early stage this transnational activity is at when compared to activity on the national level.

Tactically, traditional passive measures predominate when compared to the utilization of each other "form" (instead of the totality of activity) at the international level. Information exchange (passive) is still the leading form of coordination and joint collective bargaining (active) ranks lowest. At the national level collective bargaining is in the middle range (fourth). This was to be expected to some extent.

When the questionnaire was designed, it was thought that all of the tactics in the left column represented a scale of lowest to highest intensity of international strategic tactics. Joint collective bargaining was inserted in the middle of the scale with the full belief that it should be last. This was a check on the accuracy of the data. At this point it can be confirmed that the column can be considered a scale of present activity by shifting joint collective bargaining to the last position.

The primary criticism of international labor efforts vis-a-vis the MNC is that, with very few exceptions, there has been no collective bargaining across national borders. These data refute that position because, although joint collective bargaining ranks least in their level of activity, 31.6 percent of those who chose to answer the question indicated they had engaged in that. One should not make too much of this, however, because of differing definitions of what constitutes bargaining as well as the unverified nature of these claims. On the other hand, however, even if we include the "missing" and look at the percentage of total respondents (who number 56) who positively indicated they engaged in joint collective bargaining, the percentage (21.4 percent) is still high.

The national rank order of labor activity vis-a-vis the MNC is different than the international order and does not form a scale as per the original questionnaire's left column. Scheduled joint meetings occur more frequently than irregular consultation does. As the opposite is true at the international level, it can be assumed that international labor action is of a more informal nature at the passive stage. It is more difficult, and expensive, to conduct formal meetings internationally than locally.

The effort to influence legislation is a more useful tactic nationally because international legal bodies, such as the European Parliament, are weak with little authority and attempts by foreign unions to influence national legislatures could be viewed as a hostile act. An attempt to influence occurred recently, from the management perspective, when the U.S. Chamber of Commerce tried to influence the German parliament not to enact the new law on codetermination. The backlash was heavy against the United States and the MNCs in Germany.

It is noteworthy that sympathy strikes are presently used more as an international tactic than as a national device. Although some countries do outlaw international sympathy strikes, they are often conducted with disregard of the law. As an international weapon, they are extremely effective, but difficult to organize. Thirty-eight percent of those responding indicated that they had used international sympathy strikes internationally compared with 57.9 percent nationally. The rank order, however (fourth international, sixth national), leads one to believe that, although it is used less frequently compared to national usage, it is used more often within the total context of international activity. See Table 3.13.

Strike fund assistance, another extremely effective weapon in labor's arsenal, followed a similar pattern to sympathy strike—higher international use than national. Because this indicates financial resources being given to support union coffers, primarily through international trade secretariats, it is an indication that international labor activity against the MNC is taken seriously by trade unions—beyond establishing position platforms. Of course, a greater indication would be details on financial support. Unfortunately, such information is not available.

Certain specific comments were made with respect to the MNC that also help to clarify the previously mentioned data:

### United Kingdom

U.K. unions stressed their primary concern with national priorities. The Northern Carpet Union was an exception. However, the Society of Graphic and Allied Trades said it would engage in sympathy

**TABLE 3.13**    Transnational Activity: MNC Versus General

|  | MNC International Activity | Total International Activity |
|---|---|---|
|  | Rank | Rank |
| Exchange of information | 1 | 1 |
| Irregular consultation | 2 | 2 |
| Scheduled joint meetings | 3 | 3 |
| Attempt to influence a legislative body | 4 | 5 |
| Strike fund assistance | 5 | 4 |
| Sympathy strike | 6 | 6 |
| Joint collective bargaining | 7 | 7 |

The only disparity between these two rank orders is with "attempt to influence a legislative body" and "strike fund assistance." As the difference is only 1.9 percent, it can be assumed that they are extremely close. Thus the total energies of the international labor movement apparently coincide with its particular international efforts directed against the MNC.

action against an MNC, but only be in support of U.K. workers. A Scottish mining union said it was aware of international consultation or bargaining on cost of living clauses, but would not say where.

The British Post Office Management's Staff Association, a white-collar union, did say that in 1974 it refused to handle mail destined to France because of a strike by French postal workers. The Postal Trade Secretariat (PTTI) "ordered" it not to work and it "obeyed." Furthermore, it supported the Canadian postal strike in 1974.*

The Association of Broadcasting Staff in London indicated it had requested a policy-procedural change in another country and had used international representative assistance from its ITS in bargaining. Both of these were "confidential" and it would not indicate details of either. It did point out that it had reached international agreement on a managements rights issue over filming of coproductions.

The Association of Cinematograph Television and Allied Technicians stated that it had been involved in confidential requests for procedural changes in some countries, had used international representatives, and had received international financial assistance. Furthermore, it had been involved in international action against Dunlop/Pirelli and Kodak in support of workers in France and Italy. It had also engaged in sympathy strikes supporting Irish workers.

---

*Letter from J. Lovelady, research officer, U.K. Post Office Management's Staff Association, February 12, 1975.

## Other Countries

Although there were responses from other countries, it was primarily from the United Kingdom that written comments were received in addition to the information called for on the first page. Many of the French responses were marked "confidential" stating that they were "negotiating" to utilize some of the international tactics described in the questionnaire. Two of these responses came from unions associated with the CGC (General Confederation of Cadres), so some credence should be given to it as they confirm each other's position. Furthermore, one union federation, the Textile Workers in France, said that it sent its affiliates the questionnaire but did not receive a response.

The International Metalworkers Federation response is of note, as it was completed by its president, Daniel Benedict. As he is one of the most important figures in international labor activity, his answers are of particular interest. He indicated that the IMF had either consulted or bargained for benefits in the Caribbean bauxite and Latin American automobile industries. The IMF had used bargaining gains in one settlement as leverage in another "too often to list." Although Benedict thought that international sympathy strikes were rare, he pointed to Italian port workers going out in sympathy with Spanish and Polish shipbuilding workers. As the questionnaire calls for tactics used by "your union," it is unclear how the IMF would have become involved in this. The IMF also had sent international representatives to General Electric and International Harvester negotiations, and has supported General Electric strikes in Spain through organized consumer boycotts in 1969.

Benedict's comments are far-ranging. He took great care in filling out the questionnaire, commenting that the "meaning was not clear" to him about certain questions. His responses appear to confirm the major role the literature gives to the IMF in transnational labor activity (described in Chapter 2).

Gunter Kopke of the European Metalworkers, the regional organization of Benedict's IMF, was more circumspect by not answering many questions, but he did indicate that it had supported overtime stoppages within the same MNC between countries. Kopke indicated that the IMF has a "collective bargaining committee which meets several times a year, at which information is exchanged by the different national organizations on the claims, gains or course of negotiations in the different countries, *so that certainly one country is influenced by what is being achieved in another."*

---

*Letter from Gunter Kopke, European Metalworkers, September 11, 1974 (emphasis added).

The Stuttgart Transport Workers indicated that it had participated in "navigation" sympathy strikes. The Stuttgart workers and the IMF thus demonstrated that workers who at best have remote interests with workers outside their industry are actively engaging in strike action internationally.

The CGT of Luxembourg, a major central trade union body, also indicated that it had bargained or consulted across national borders on a number of issues and had refused to work overtime in support of workers in the same MNC. It did not indicate where.

The Danish Metalworkers stated that "MNC's in Denmark are the most advanced and best paying companies. National companies make much more trouble."* This is the only positive comment received from a union about MNCs, although compensation surveys in many countries do indicate that MNCs, particularly U.S., wish to remain "good corporate citizens" and avoid union difficulties by paying at or above market. Therefore, it is somewhat surprising that only one union mentioned this.

The Belgian Metalworkers specifically mentioned international consultation or bargaining at Phillips, Siemens, Ford, and Foxol. Another Belgian union, the WCL Affiliated Metalworkers, also indicated activity at Phillips between Belgium and the Netherlands. The Dutch CNV (Central National Christian Workers Federation) stated that it had supported sympathy strikes at Akzo in 1972 (see Chapter 2) and had engaged in managements rights consultation or bargaining assistance at Hoogovens-Hoechst in Estel, West Germany.

### Geographic Distribution of Responses

Table 3.14 indicates the extent of national and international activity by country in those countries where three or more unions responded. I am reluctant to draw conclusions or indicate trends from these data because the number of respondents per country is small. In those countries where three or more unions answered the questionnaire, I tabulated the total number of "yes" responses and found the percentage of these in the total of all categories (exchange of information to sympathy strikes). Thus no conclusion can be reached about which form of activity is more prevalent in a single country. However, one can look at the general level of activity vis-a-vis the MNC with the view that the data are open to question because of the small sample.

Certain speculations and subsequent observations are in order:

---

*Questionnaire response from Danish Metalworkers.

1. Denmark, like other Scandinavian countries, has a highly central-ized labor movement, which, through the NFS, has developed a cohesive policy on MNCs.
2. Belgium has the highest concentration of MNCs in the Common Market.[3] It is thus noteworthy that this country has the second highest level of activity. The concentration of MNCs, particularly U.S., may have been a spur to this activity.
3. Switzerland has a more decentralized, and weaker, labor move-ment than many European countries, although it is the headquar-ters of some major MNCs, for example, Nestle. Because only three unions responded from Switzerland, no conclusions should be drawn, although their high level of MNC activity is interesting.
4. The French labor movement is the most complex of the five. It is a combination of centralized labor movements with a plethora of activity at the local or plant level. The French are, according to these data, vigorously pursuing MNC activity at the national level. At the international level their activity falls off. However, I would suspect that in certain categories, for example, exchange of infor-mation, they are active.
5. The U.K. labor movement is the most decentralized of the five (similar to the U.S.); however, as noted in Chapter 2, the TUC is actively pursuing an international policy. It had a high response level; thus, the data are of some interest here. This high level of international activity (and national) does confirm that the TUC has taken its efforts beyond formal positions.

## MNC Responses

The primary concentration of this book is to examine transnational union behavior. It was originally thought that MNC responses to a questionnaire would be an interesting test of how valid the union responses were. The basic question was: Did MNCs also indicate that they had engaged in a transnational effort with a union so claiming? Did their overall perceptions match that of the unions?

One hundred and thirty-two companies were sent questionnaires. Only 16 returned the questionnaires, although many sent letters asking for the results of the study or expressed great interest. One company has written four times asking for the completed work based upon a small amount of information it supplied in a letter. Many companies said they could not disclose information because it was not "their pol-icy" or, more interestingly, the legal structures of their companies did not so permit. Their claim was that the corporate veil would not permit communication with subsidiaries.

The difficulty in obtaining information tends to verify the unions' contention that company information is most difficult to get on a trans-

**TABLE 3.14**  Country Activity Level

| | National | | | International | |
|---|---|---|---|---|---|
| Country | Percent "Yes" | Sample Size | Country | Percent "Yes" | Sample Size |
| Denmark | 92.3 | 5 | Denmark | 67.8 | 5 |
| Belgium | 81.8 | 6 | Switzerland | 62.5 | 3 |
| Switzerland | 64.7 | 3 | Belgium | 55.2 | 7 |
| France | 55.5 | 6 | France | 36.6 | 5 |
| United Kingdom | 52.3 | 8 | United Kingdom | 34.1 | 7 |

Note: Percentages are of total "yes" responses versus all responses throughout each category in either international or national columns.

national basis. This is why disclosure of information is written into many of their position statements on MNCs and is part of some laws on codetermination.

As the company responses received were such a small sample, I thought it better to indicate what was said in some specific responses rather than to attempt statistical analysis. Trans World Airlines said that there was frequent exchange of information and irregular consultation by unions about it between countries. Furthermore, it engaged in the same practice with other companies (probably through employer federations), although no joint collective bargaining has been held. It has had bargaining gains in one country used for leverage purposes in France and Italy as well as transnational sympathy strikes in those countries. Furthermore, the workers in the United Kingdom refused to work overtime in support of TWA workers in another country. TWA stated: "Basically, unions in our experience are trying to coordinate their efforts by the type of business and not as an attack on the entire company."* TWA expects "more and more without question" transnational cooperation among unions.

E. I. Du Pont de Nemours & Company, another major company organized by unions of the ICF, indicated "seldom" to the first three categories of "MNC between the countries" and "seldom" to sympathy strike in that category. Furthermore, it has participated with other companies on labor strategy in the EEC, Switzerland, and Sweden.

Imperial Chemicals (ICI), a major U.K. multinational, has had less transnational labor activity than either Kaiser or Du Pont according to its questionnaire responses. A letter from its management said, "It is

---

*Letter from Mr. Connors, manager, Labor Relations Administration, Trans World Airlines, Oakland, Calif., September 20, 1974.

our firm policy that employment relationships should be determined in accordance with good practice and laws of each country, and that the international company should not try to interfere in this process from any central position."* This is an excellent summary of the MNCs' policy on transnational labor—"local practice must prevail." However, ICI still indicated irregular consultation and information exchange against it by trade unions. It did note that Monsanto in both the United Kingdom and Europe had received international representative assistance from the ICF; however, it thought that the national unions in the chemicals industry did not often support these attacks.

Exxon thought "many unions attempt to influence legislation, some across national boundaries (IMF and ICF)." They also said that it was only at the information exchange and irregular consultation levels that unions had been active transnationally against them. Exxon had participated in the same activity, including joint meetings, but had not engaged in joint collective bargaining. One key point is that Exxon has had bargaining gains in one settlement used in another in "most countries" and federation assistance has been given to its unions in Latin America.

Kaiser Aluminum indicated a great deal of transnational activity against it. This would tend to confirm Levinson's contention that the ICF has been extremely active transnationally.[4] Kaiser responded "frequently" to the first six questions under "within the MNC between countries." As two of these are active categories (joint collective bargaining and scheduled joint meetings), this is a significant finding because it is a level of specific activity that has, to my knowledge, never been documented.

Kaiser is the only company to indicate that it had engaged in collective bargaining on a transnational basis. Furthermore, bargaining gains made in one country have been used as leverage in another in Ghana and Jamaica. It believes this is a "standard union tactic." International union representatives are "used consistently" and the negotiation of worldwide common expiration dates is a normal union demand.

The Continental Oil Company circled "C" (confidential), which has been interpreted as a "yes" for most transnational categories through number five (see Appendix). Thus, it also indicates transnational collective bargaining but does not indicate where.

Control Data stated that, although it thought transnational bargaining or consultation had occurred in Germany (on management rights) and productivity clauses (United Kingdom), information picketing to reduce sales had been directed against it in the United States and Eu-

---

*Letter from J. Coates, general manager, Personnel, Du Pont, October 31, 1974.

rope, as well as transnational consumer boycotts and overtime refusal. In Europe it has been confronted with demands for common expiration dates. Hertz Corporation indicated minimal transnational activity, although it participates in exchanging information with other companies in the United Kingdom on labor matters. Brown Boveri, a major German MNC, indicated joint meetings and information exchange against it between countries by unions, but it had never been confronted with specific tactics.

As Akzo is a major case in the literature, I was pleased to receive a reply from the company. As could be expected, Akzo confirmed what the literature tells us, that there is "frequent" joint collective bargaining, and it had experienced strike fund assistance and sympathy strikes in Holland. However, it did not indicate that there was extensive cooperation among countries against it.

Royal Dutch Shell in a letter stated, "As far as Shell in the Netherlands is concerned, the biggest Dutch union federation (NVV) has promised Mr. Charles Levinson, Secretary General of the ICF, to contribute to the institution of a data bank on Shell's conditions of service and policies all over the world for the use of the so-called 'Royal Dutch Shell Permanent World Council.' "* One wonders why Shell would accede to Levinson's request to supply valuable information to a data bank if it has had "no contacts with the Council." Perhaps it believes this is a way of delaying joint transnational discussion; however, it is doubtful that this strategy will work once it has given the ICF the raw data to work with.

Shell Netherlands of Rotterdam was forwarded a copy of the questionnaire by the head office, and it indicated transnational activity, including "scheduled joint meetings" directed against it.

General Electric indicated that a significant amount of transnational labor activity had been directed toward it. This included strike fund assistance and sympathy strikes, although no bargaining on a transnational basis had occurred. General Electric frequently met with other companies to exchange information and consult on labor matters, although it would not state which countries.

One company that strongly indicated it did not wish to be identified but will be at this point, General Foods, said that questions 19 through 27 in the questionnaire should be generally answered "yes."† It was extremely cautious and did not give further details, but it is known that the IUF, the International Trade Secretariat for Foodwork-

---

*Letter from H. Van Schendel, Shell Nederland B. V., December 18, 1974.

†Letter from Paul Grehl, director, Employee Relations, General Foods, White Plains, N.Y., September 16, 1974.

ers, has claimed numerous successes. This would appear to confirm its claim at at least one major MNC—General Foods.

## SUMMARY

What can now be said about the extent of international labor activity: Let us return to our original questions:

1. What is the form in which these transactions occur?

More than 60 percent of the unions responding exchange information, have irregular consultations, and schedule joint meetings. Although the lowest level of rank order of international activity is joint collective bargaining, a surprising 20 percent indicated this had occurred in their experience. Strike fund assistance, sympathy strikes, and efforts to influence legislation on a transnational basis were in the 41 to 48 percent range.

2. Are different forms of labor activity utilized depending upon whether activity is national or transnational?

Yes, and with less frequency at the international level. Exchange of information is the area that is conducted primarily at both levels. However, there is a 17 percent lag internationally. Joint collective bargaining at the national level—unions combining their strength against a specific employer—is far more common at the national level. Legislative influence is not only more common nationally but a more acceptable practice than at the international level.

3. Is there a significant level of transnational activity directed specifically against the MNC? How intense is it?

Transnational labor activity against the MNC was in the 60 to 75 percent range for those who responded (of 56 respondents, no more than 16 in any one category did not respond) for the first three categories. One of these is considered "active"—scheduled joint meetings. Although the data from the corporations are far from conclusive because of the small sample, it should be noted that they too perceived a cutoff of activity at that point. As this activity is quite specifically directed toward MNCs, one can conclude that transnational labor relations in Europe is at an incipient stage. Since 40 of the 56 unions are trade union centers, this may appear to be a new development. National trade union centers are charged with labor activity only for that country, usually within an ideological or religious context. The trend appears to be that national centers perceive their self-interest as, at least to some extent, being beyond their borders. This has been precipitated by the MNC because it has encouraged these national centers to work jointly on an MNC strategy.

International MNC coordination never fell below the 30 percent frequency level. Joint collective bargaining was in the lowest order of activity ranking. However, a 31.6 percent response of those answering and a 21.4 percent response rate of the total union questionnaires returned indicating that international collective bargaining had occurred is significant because a contrary recurrent theme occurs in the literature. This is that international collective bargaining has only occurred in a few instances; indeed, some management questionnaires said this. However, even accounting for different definitions of transnational bargaining, the previously mentioned percentages are much higher than original expectations based upon a reading of the literature. This may be a fruitful area for further study.

International sympathy action (37.8 percent), while relatively low, is also at a high frequency. This appears to be a fruitful area for future transnational activity by unions.

Strike fund assistance ranked fifth as an international tactic vis-a-vis the MNCs. Financial commitment is extremely important for unions to gain strength. As it can be expected that most of the money is channeled through international trade secretariats, it is possible that it may not appear on their balances. Indeed, it is quite possible that various national unions channel money through ITSs to other national unions. This is a convenient way for a union not to become directly involved.

The totality of activity as measured by the questionnaire results indicates that there are more active transactions than passive ones at the international level directed against MNCs. This is the reverse of what occurs at the national level for reasons already stated. Thus international labor transactions are of an active nature, they are high in frequency, specifically directed to MNCs, and their tactics are about the same as those utilized in general (non-MNC-directed) international labor relations.

## NOTES

1. "IMF Systematic Analysis of Multinational Companies Worldwide and at Subsidiary Level, I. The Ford Motor Company," Geneva, Switzerland, October 1974, p. 3.

2. H. Northrup and R. Rowan, "Multinational Union-Management Consultation: The European Experience," *Institute of Labor Review* 116, no. 2 (September-October 1977): 154.

3. "Special Report on Multinational Companies," *Fortune,* August 1973, p. 146.

4. H. Northrup and R. Rowan, "Multinational Collective Bargaining: The Factual Record in Chemicals, Glass, and Rubber Tires. Pt. II," *Columbia Journal of World Business* (Summer 1974): 49–62.

# 4 TRADE UNION RESPONSE TO MULTINATIONALS: an analysis

In Chapter 2 the role of interest groups was reviewed in terms of their importance to the process of political integration. Additionally, it was seen that political integration does not have a standard definition in political science literature. The tenet of the communications theorists, that integration is a process, was therefore accepted. It was also determined that there would be some utility to examining concepts from each of the integrationist schools, such as spillover and community. The methodology would rely primarily upon Karl Deutsch's concept of transactions across national borders as an indicator of community and a potential step in the integration process. Beyond this, the literature of political science was not helpful because of its concern with the state-centric paradigm. The state was seen to be at the core of political science, including Deutsch's own concept of core for political integration.

Labor relations as an issue area for state action has been examined by testing how transnational this interest group has become. Utilizing the communications concept of transactions, it was seen in the previous chapters that transactions in various forms were numerous and more active transnationally than nationally. The MNC was viewed as a primary motivating force for these transactions after examining the relevant frameworks (Marxist, minor impact, and liberal-functionalist) concerning the MNC. It was concluded that all frameworks were found to need further analysis to determine how to utilize best empirical data, but it was primarily the liberal-functionalist view that perceived MNCs as a motivating force.

The data indicate an active, and growing, international labor movement in Europe. Although the United Kingdom appears to be somewhat isolated, part of which may be attributed to its different industrial relations system, there nevertheless is an increasing transnational integration of industrial relations practices. The cause, to some extent, is the MNC, although other areas beyond the scope of this work could be tested, such as the impact of economic integration of the various European nations. Almost all of the responses from Scandinavia (a highly integrated area) indicated much transnational activity primarily through its regional body, the NFS, and also through the remainder of Europe.

The framework for transnational labor relations is well developed. Information exchange occurs broadly across union organizational lines and between countries. Seventy-five percent of the unions responding indicated they exchanged transnational information about MNCs. Thus unions affiliated with the same company in France and perhaps Germany regularly traded information. This is an astoundingly high rate of transaction, as the communications theorists would term it.

The conclusion of the review of data on transnational labor relations is that transnational activity in the form of specific action against the MNC is more prevalent than has previously been disclosed. Utilizing the criteria of the communications school, which sees "lines between people as very important, regardless of national boundaries,"[1] it is apparent that an international community is in the process of development, at least within Europe.

This conclusion is somewhat contrary to Robert Cox's belief that it "would be difficult for Swedish trade unions, for example, to take part in transnationally coordinated action against a particular corporation as this would probably violate the agreements concluded for the whole industry by the central trade union movement."[2] The data in Chapter 4 demonstrate that unions have been able to overcome, at least to a certain point, their organizational problems in dealing with MNCs on a transnational basis. Cox is more accurate when he notes that the structure of European trade unionism (a combination of decentralization for local agreements and "traditionally centralized" collective bargaining) has "strengthened the basis for a company by company approach to industrial relations which could lend itself to transnational coordination."[3]

Joseph Nye, Charles Levinson of the ICF, and R. J. Barnet and R. E. Muller all speak of the "global character" of the MNC.[4] Nye indicates that "their [the MNC] effects on world trade and production can be judged by the fact that the production of overseas subsidiaries of the ten leading capital exporting states was nearly twice the volume of trade between those countries."[5] The importance of MNCs to the world economy in view of these three observers is therefore extremely significant. Indeed, Levinson believes that MNCs are the "first genuine world institutions with inherently global power and authority. Since nation-states do not control the operation of corporations, unions must urgently create a countervailing force. This can be done by transnational coordination of bargaining and also by participation of union representatives in management."[6]

My approach has been to review the impact of the MNC on transnational industrial relations within the total context of European labor relations. One can see, as the neofunctionalists have, that MNCs and their linkages have had a spillover on other political forces in the form of interest groups, for example, labor unions. This impact has created a transnational linkage of trade unions, primarily among their leaders, but also to some extent their rank and file. The self-interest of these unions as demonstrated by these transactions is linked to the transnational economy of the world.

National authority is losing its position as the primary source for trade union interests. The first recognition of this was when trade unions saw a need to protect minimal standards such as wages on a worldwide basis. This was done through the ILO and usually ratified by member governments. The MNC, however, has brought an entirely new dimension to this. Trade unions now look to themselves, to use Levinson's words, to form a "countervailing force." In their view, national authority has not been able to control satisfactorily MNC policies that affect labor matters.

The impact of transnational labor relations for political integration analysis is noteworthy. Looking to a new paradigm in political science, one that deemphasizes the role of the state and increases emphasis upon interest-group behavior, one can see certain developments:

1. Utilizing the method of the communications school by measuring transactions across national borders, it can be seen that trade unions are developing an international community primarily in Western Europe but with links to the United States and to a lesser extent the developing countries.

2. The concept of state loyalty should be examined as a result of these transnational linkages. Although it is not foreseeable that loyalty to the trade union will achieve more importance than that of the state, it is quite probable that union power will increase as the impact of the MNC spreads and becomes more known to the rank and file. This is a long-term trend. Even at this point, one could question if primary loyalty of the U.K. rank and file is to the trade union movement or the state. However, this does not appear to be related to direct transnational issues.

3. The ability of the state to control its own economy becomes more questionable in the global economy. The impact of OPEC on

inflation, as well as the result of certain states (primarily Middle Eastern) buying large shares of MNCs, demonstrates that in the future states may not only lose control but headquarters control of the MNC itself may be loosened.

4. Trade unions are developing their own communications network, and may utilize the threats of international sympathy strikes and transnational collective bargaining as vehicles for overcoming weakened state power. They will, in short, resort to their own resources. The resort to union transnational power networks is a reflection to some extent of the state's inability to control the MNC. Indeed the criticism by the ICFTU of MNCs in third-world countries (see Chapter 2) is a criticism of the home country's lack of effectiveness of control of subsidiaries in foreign countries. State control where it is tightest, in third-world countries, usually works to the benefit of MNCs because wages are kept low to attract investment.

5. Ratification by European nations and the United States of various codes on MNCs, such as that recently issued by the OECD, is looked to with optimism by trade unions. It is thought that these codes could prove to be an effective device for curbing MNC power. However, if the curbs are only minimal, one could expect the trade unions to increase efforts for transnational bargaining. Once again, this is an extension of the idea of countervailing power to the MNCs. If the nation-state fails to do it, the trade unions will try to do it for themselves.

6. Organizationally, the trade unions are disregarding their ideological divisions by merging to meet the needs of the transnational economy. Within Europe the Christian and liberal federations have merged to form the European Trade Union Congress. The international trade secretariats are establishing regional offshoots of their central organizations. The primary example of this is the European Metalworkers Federation, a regional body of the IMF.

7. Robert Koehane and Nye note Stanley Hoffman's distinction between "high politics" and "low politics."[7] Their studies of transnational relations show that "issue areas that were formally quite distinct from political calculation have become politically relevant, particularly insofar as governments have attempted to extend their control over domestic economic activity without sacrificing the benefits of transnational intercourse."[8] The labor issue area as a key component of international economic activity must now be calculated into this equation. International trade and economic dependency, especially within highly integrated economic regions such as the EEC, are either increased or decreased as a result of labor's actions.

In those industries that are highly integrated across economic borders, transnational labor activity becomes even more effective. The

U.K. automobile industry is in reality highly dependent upon Belgian and German parts. The United Kingdom and most other developed countries consider automobiles a cornerstone of the economy and to some extent a factor affecting political stability. Labor's transnational power in this industry, while already at a highly developed state, is increasing. If present trends continue, labor will be able to be as well integrated as the automobile MNCs themselves. A recent example is the recent Chrysler experience in the United Kingdom, which led to an unprecedented bailout for a U.K. company. It was precipitated by U.K. unions with active European IMF affiliate support. The potential impact of this is significant because the ultimate conclusion is that a well-developed transnational MNC labor network could have world-wide political impact.

8. The development of transnational labor relations as a political issue area is occurring without a supranational authority. It is somewhat informal and spurred by central organizations.

As noted, there are numerous international organizations, including the ILO. However, it is the 16 ITSs that have been the initiators of transnational communications. The transnational network developed functionally within each industry for major MNCs and is a response to their globalization. The network arose from a basic trade union need —to countervail power—and did not arise from a central power source. The ITSs were organizationally best equipped to meet this need, as they are global centers organized on industry lines. They initiated, but the true power centers—national trade union bodies—have responded and maintained the network. It is for this reason that the network has not been easy to pinpoint. There is no central source of power. Thus the value of communications methodology, the utilization of a frequency count of transactions, has proven to be invaluable.

Communications analysis has permitted this author to perceive a latent European community of workers, which to some extent (and this is not conclusive) has been a reaction to the MNCs. Thus, within the context of communications theory, an essential step for the formation of a politically integrated Europe is occurring—the development of community.

The implications of this for policy makers in MNCs who may perceive state boundaries as an irrelevant anachronism (Harold Geneen, former chief executive officer at ITT viewed states in this manner) are substantial, although long-term. It is they who will have to deal with corporate policies that address employees as workers who perceive their interests extending beyond their own plant to another across a national border—particularly if it is part of the same company. This is not to say that transnational labor activity by its very nature is inimical to the MNC; indeed, it may be quite the opposite. This becomes apparent when examining the labor culture of northern Europe with its emphasis upon codetermination with management.

As I view transnational labor integration as a five- to ten-year phenomenon, far-sighted companies will be able to adapt well-planned strategies, just as the unions have been doing. In essence, the unions have gone one step at a time, not necessarily viewing transnational collective bargaining as an end. MNCs will have to address these strategies in the same methodical manner, beginning with their own exchange of information across national borders about labor/personnel relations. The effect of these transnational activities will then be brought to bear upon the nation-state. As this occurs, more concrete indications of political integration as a response to transnational labor activity will be evident.

## NOTES

1. Deutsch, *Nationalism and Its Alternatives.*

2. Robert W. Cox, "Labor and Transnational Relations," in *Transnational Relations and World Politics,* ed. Robert O. Koehane and Joseph S. Nye, Jr., (Cambridge, Mass.: Harvard University Press, 1972), p. 217.

3. Ibid., p. 213.

4. Joseph S. Nye and Robert Koehane, "Transnational Relations and World Politics" in ibid.; Charles Levinson, *Industry's Democratic Revolution* (London: Allen & Unwin, 1974); R. J. Barnet and R. E. Muller, *Global Reach—The Power of the Multinational Corporations* (New York: Simon & Schuster, 1974).

5. Nye, ibid., p. 377.

6. Charles Levinson, "Towards Industrial Democracy," as quoted in his statement delivered to the First International Trade Union Conference on Industrial Democracy, Frankfurt, West Germany, November 28–29, 1968. This text has been reprinted in the *ICF Bulletin,* January 1969, special issue.

7. Robert O. Koehane and Joseph S. Nye, Jr., eds., *Transnational Relations and World Politics* (Cambridge, Mass.: Harvard University Press, 1972), pp. 378–79.

8. Ibid., p. 379.

# APPENDIX

## UNIONS RESPONDING TO QUESTIONNAIRE

| Location | Name |
| --- | --- |
| Brussels | National Confederation of Cadres |
| Paris | Sindicat Nacional des Travailleurs Sucrocrere (CGC) |
| Brussels | Christian Confederation of Public Service Unions (CSC) |
| Halifax (U.K.) | Northern Carpet Trade Union |
| Paris | Textile Workers Federation of France |
| Brussels | World Federation of Workers in Food, Tobacco and Hotel Industries (International Trade Secretariat) |
| Paris | National Federation of Cadre Unions for Chemical, Pharmaceutical and Connected Industries (CGC— General Cadre Confederation) |
| Malaysia | Malaysian Trade Union Congress |
| Nice (France) | Autonomous Unions of Succursales de L'Agence Havas |
| Brussels | Central Union for Book and Paper Industry |
| Luxembourg | CGT |
| Djakarta (Indonesia) | Federation of Indonesian Islamic Trade Unions (GASBINBO) |
| Colombo (Sri Lanka) | National Workers Congress |
| Paris | National Federation of Agricultural Workers and Connected Sectors (FO) |
| Amsterdam (Netherlands) | Dutch Trade Union Confederation (NVV) |
| Geneva | International Metal Workers Federation (International Trade Secretariat) |
| Finland | Confederation of Salaried Employees in Finland (TVK) |
| United States | AFL–CIO |
| Denmark | Danish Metal Workers |
| Sweden | Swedish Trade Union Confederation (LO) |
| Brussels | International Textile Garment and Leather Workers Federation (ITS) |
| Switzerland | National Federation of Musicians (ITS) |
| Spain | Province of Guipuzcca Trade Unions |
| Bern (Switzerland) | Union Suisse Syndicale |
| Bern (Switzerland) | Union Suisse Syndicale (second response) |
| Stuttgart (Germany) | Transport Workers Union |
| Brussels | Belgian Central Christian Metallurgists |
| Utrecht (Netherlands) | National Christian Workers Federation |
| Nigeria | United Labor Congress |
| Denmark | Diversified Danish Trade Union Federation |
| Finland | Finnish Trade Unions (SAK) |
| Hamburg (Germany) | DAG |

(continued)

98

## UNIONS RESPONDING TO QUESTIONNAIRE (Continued)

| Location | Name |
|---|---|
| Denmark | LO |
| Denmark | Danish Metal Workers (second response) |
| Utrecht (Netherlands) | World Federation of Wood and Building Workers (ITS) (blank questionnaire returned due to no interaction with multinationals) |
| Switzerland | European Metal Workers (partially filled in with no explanation) |
| Brussels | Confederation of Christian Unions (blank questionnaire) |
| India | All India Trade Union Congress |
| Brussels | World Federation for the Metallurgic Industry (WCL) |
| Kassel (West Germany) | Gewerkschaft Gartenbau Land-und Forstwirtschaft |
| France | Syndicat National des Cadres des Administrateurs de Biens (CGC) (Managers of Goods) |
| France | Union Syndicale de la Maitrise du Petrole (USMAP) |
| Copenhagen (Denmark) | Handels—OG Kontorfunktionaerernes Forbund I Denmark (LO) |
| Great Britain | Electrical Electronic Telecommunication and Plumbing Union |
| France | |
| United States | United Auto Workers, Washington, D.C. |
| Belgium | Christian Syndicate of Railways, Post, Telephone, Shipping, Aviation, Radio and Television |
| Great Britain | Association of Scientific, Technical and Managerial Staffs |
| Belgium | World Federation of Agricultural Workers |
| Great Britain | Sheffield Sawmakers Protection Society |
| Great Britain | Society of Graphical and Allied Trades |
| Scotland | Colliery Overmen, Deputies and Shot Firers, National Association (mining) |
| Great Britain | Post Office Management Staff's Association |
| Great Britain | Association of Broadcasting Staff |
| Scotland | Electrical Power Engineers' Association |
| Great Britain | Association of Cinematograph Television and Allied Technicians |

# SAMPLE QUESTIONS

MULTINATIONAL CORPORATIONS AND TRADE UNIONS:
EMERGING TRENDS AND IMPLICATIONS FOR THE NATION–STATE

<u>KEY</u>

MNC = MULTINATIONAL CORPORATION
N = NEVER
S = SELDOM
F = FREQUENTLY
C = CONFIDENTIAL

TRADE UNION QUESTIONNAIRE
©COPYRIGHT BY PAUL WEINBERG
1974

## I. COOPERATION

Indicate extent of Cooperation with Other Unions, Syndicates or Federations by circling N (never), S (seldom), or F (frequently), or C (Confidential). Additional comment is appreciated.

| | Another Plant or Office in Same Geographic Area | MNC Within the Country | Within the MNC Between Countries | Within Federation in Your Country | Cross-Federation but Within Country | Cross-Federation and Between Countries | |
|---|---|---|---|---|---|---|---|
| 1. Exchange of information | N S F C | N S F C | N S F C | N S F C | N S F C | N S F C | 1 |
| 2. Irregular consultation | N S F C | N S F C | N S F C | N S F C | N S F C | N S F C | 2 |
| 3. Scheduled joint meetings | N S F C | N S F C | N S F C | N S F C | N S F C | N S F C | 3 |
| 4. Joint collective bargaining | N S F C | N S F C | N S F C | N S F C | N S F C | N S F C | 4 |
| 5. Attempt to influence a legislative body | N S F C | N S F C | N S F C | N S F C | N S F C | N S F C | 5 |
| 6. Support for legislation in another country that could affect your employment (protectionist trade policies) | | | | | | | |
| 7. Strike fund assistance | N S F C | N S F C | N S F C | N S F C | N S F C | N S F C | 6 |
| 8. Sympathy strike | N S F C | N S F C | N S F C | N S F C | N S F C | N S F C | 7 |
| | N S F C | N S F C | N S F C | N S F C | N S F C | N S F C | 8 |

100

## II. BARGAINING OR CONSULTATION ACROSS NATIONAL BOUNDARIES

Has this occured to your knowledge:

|  | Already Occurred (State Where) | Doubtful | Probable |  |
|---|---|---|---|---|
| 9. Wages |  |  |  | 9 |
| 10. Productivity clauses |  |  |  | 10 |
| 11. Cost of living clauses |  |  |  | 11 |
| 12. Management rights (codetermination) |  |  |  | 12 |
| 13. Benefits |  |  |  | 13 |
| 14. Other |  |  |  | 14 |

## III. BARGAINING TACTICS

Have any of the following tactics been used by your union?

|  | No | Yes | Where | Confidential |  |
|---|---|---|---|---|---|
| 15. Request for a policy or procedural change in another country |  |  |  |  | 15 |
| 16. Information picketing to reduce sales in another country or another plant or an MNC within the country |  |  |  |  | 16 |
| 17. Use of bargaining gain in one settlement as leverage in another country |  |  |  |  | 17 |
| 17-A. Has this occurred within the same MNC? |  |  |  |  | 17-A |
| 18. Sympathy strikes in support of workers in another country |  |  |  |  | 18 |
| 19. Refusal to work overtime in support of a work stoppage in the same MNC or another country |  |  |  |  | 19 |
| 20. Consumer boycotts |  |  |  |  | 20 |
| 21. Negotiation of common expiration dates |  |  |  |  | 21 |
| 22. Use of federation or international representative assistance in bargaining |  |  |  |  | 22 |
| 23. Receipt of financial assistance from a federation, union, or trade secretariat outside your country |  |  |  |  | 23 |

Please state your opinions about the future for cooperation between unions (including U.S.-European ties), particularly with respect to multinationals as well as any management coordination of which you are aware.

101

# BIBLIOGRAPHY

Alger, Chadwick F. "The Multinational Corporations and the Future International System." *Annals of the American Academy of Political and Social Science* 403 (September 1972): 104–15.

Almond, Gabriel A., and Coleman, J., eds. *The Politics of the Developing Areas.* Princeton, N.J.: Princeton University Press, 1960.

Almond, Gabriel A., and Powell, G. *Comparative Politics: A Developmental Approach.* Boston: Little, Brown, 1966.

Avery, W. "The Extra-Regional Transfer of Integrative Behavior." *International Organization* 27 (Autumn 1973): 549–56.

Baranson, Jack. "Technology Transfer Through the International Firm." *American Economic Review* 60 (May 1970): 435–40.

Barnet, R. J., and Muller, R. E. *Global Reach—The Power of the Multinational Corporations.* New York: Simon & Schuster, 1974.

Behrman, Jack N. "Industrial Integration and the Multinational Enterprise." *Annals of the American Academy of Political and Social Science* 403 (September 1972): 46–57.

————. "The Multinational Enterprise: Its Initiatives and Governmental Reactions." *Journal of International Law and Economics* 6 (January 1972): 215–33.

Bergsten, C., Koehane, Robert O., and Nye, Joseph S. Jr. "International Economics and International Politics: a Framework for Analysis." *International Organization* 29 (Winter 1975): 3–36.

Berschin, H. Herbert. "Enterprises Multinationals et Integration Europeane." *Problemes de l'Europe* (Paris) 53 (1971): 31–37.

Blake, David H. "Trade Unions and the Challenge of the Multinational Corporation." *Annals of the American Academy of Political and Social Science* 403 (September 1972): 34–45.

Boddewyn, Jean, and Ashol, Kappor. "The External Relations of American Multinational Enterprises." *International Studies Quarterly* 16 (December 1972): 433–53.

Brecher, Michael. *The Foreign Policy System of Israel: Setting, Images, Process.* New Haven, Conn.: Yale University Press, 1972.

Brecher, Michael, Steinberg, B., and Stein, J. *Journal of Conflict Resolution* 13, no. 1 (March 1969).

Brenner, Michael J. *Technocratic Politics and the Functionalist Theory of European Integration.* Cornell Research Papers in International Studies, no. 7. Ithaca, N.Y.: Cornell University Press, 1969.

Brooke, Michael Z., and Remmers, H. L. *The Strategy of Multinational Enterprises; Organization and Finance.* New York: American Elsevier, 1970.

Cantori, L. J., and Spiegel, S. L. "The Analysis of Regional International Politics: The Integration Versus the Empirical Systems Approach." *International Organization* 27, no. 4 (Autumn 1973): 465–94.

Church, Frank. "Multinational Corporations. Will They Usher in a New World Order?" *Center (for the Study of Democratic Institutions) Magazine* 6 (May–June 1973): 15–18.

Clarke, R. O. "The Multinational Company: The State and International Organizations." Paper prepared for the Third World Congress of the International Industrial Relations Research Association, Geneva, September 1973.

Connell-Smith, G. *The Inter-American System.* New York: Oxford University Press, 1966.

Copp, Robert. "The Multinational Corporation and Industrial Relations. The Labor Affairs Function in a Multinational Firm." *Comparative International Industrial Relations.* Research Assoc. Series Industrial Relations.

Corbet, H., and Robertson, D., eds. *Europe's Free Trade Experiment. EFTA and Economic Integration.* London: Pergamon Press, 1970.

Coventry and District Engineering Employees Association. "Labor Relations and Employment Conditions in the EEC." U.K.: April 1972.

Cox, Robert W. In *Transnational Relations and World Politics.* Edited by Robert O. Koehane and Joseph S. Nye, Jr. Cambridge, Mass.: Harvard University Press, 1972.

———. "Labor and Transnational Relations." *International Organization* 25 (Summer 1971): 554–84.

Crispo, John. *International Unionism: A Study in Canadian-American Relations.* Toronto: McGraw-Hill, 1967.

Curtin, W., and Shepard, I. "International Labor Relations Multinational Collective Bargaining—An Illusory Concept." *Employee Relations Law Journal* 1, no. 1 (Summer 1975).

Dahl, Robert. *Who Governs?* New Haven, Conn.: Yale University Press, 1961.

Deutsch, Karl W. *Nationalism and Its Alternatives.* New York: Knopf, 1969.

————. *The Analysis of International Relations.* Englewood Cliffs, N.J.: Prentice-Hall, 1968.

————. "External Influences on the Internal Behavior of States. In *Approaches to Comparative and International Politics.* Edited by R. Barry Farrel. Evanston, Ill.: Northwestern University Press, 1966.

————. *The Nerves of Government.* New York: Free Press, 1965.

Dunning, J. H., ed. *The Multinational Enterprise.* New York: Praeger, 1972.

————. "Multinational Companies as a Political Problem." *World Today* (London) 28 (November 1972): 473–82.

————, ed. *The Multinational Enterprise.* London: Allen & Unwin, 1971.

Easton, David A. *A Framework for Political Analysis.* Englewood Cliffs, N.J.: Prentice-Hall, 1965.

EEC Information Department. "The Trade Union Movement in the EEC." Brussels, 1972.

Etzioni, A. *Studies in Social Change.* New York: Holt, Rinehart and Winston, 1966.

Fayerweather, John. "Elite Attitudes Toward Multinational Firms: A Study of Britain, Canada and France." *International Studies Quarterly* 16 (December 1972): 472–90.

Feld, W. J. *Non-Governmental Forces and World Politics: A Study of Business, Labor and Political Groups.* New York: Praeger, 1972.

Feldstein, Helen. "A Study of Transaction and Political Integration: Transnational Labour Flow Within the EEC." *Journal of Common Market Studies* (September 1967): 24–55.

Forrow, Brian D. "The Multinational Corporation in the Enlarged European Community." *Law and Contemporary Problems* 37 (Spring 1972): 306–17.

Friedrich, C. J. *Trends of Federalism in Theory and Practice.* New York: Praeger, 1968.

Gallaway, Jonathan F. "The Military Industrial Linkages of U.S.-Based Multinational Corporations." *International Studies Quarterly* 16 (December 1972): 491–510.

Gennard, John. *Multinational Corporations and British Labour: A Review of Attitudes and Responses.* London: British North American Committee, 1972.

Goodman, Elliot R. "The Impact of the Multinational Enterprise Upon the Atlantic Community." *Atlantic Community Quarterly* 10 (Fall 1972): 357–67.

Gorz, André. *Strategy for Labor: A Radical Proposal.* Translated from the French by Martin A. Nicolaus and V. Ortiz. Boston: Beacon Press, 1967.

Gunter, Hans, ed. *Transnational Industrial Relations.* London: Macmillan, 1972.

Haas, Ernst B. *Beyond the Nation-State: Functionalism and International Organization.* Stanford, Calif.: Stanford University Press, 1964.

———. *The Unity of Europe: Political, Social and Economic Forces, 1950-1957.* Stanford, Calif.: Stanford University Press, 1958.

Heise, Paul A. "The Multinational Corporation and Industrial Relations: Discussion." *Comparative International Industrial Relations.* Research Assoc., Series Industrial Relations.

Hoffman, Stanley B. *The Relevance of International Law.* Edited by Karl Deutsch and Stanley Hoffman. Cambridge, Mass.: Schenkman, 1968.

———. *Contemporary Theory in International Relations.* Englewood Cliffs, N.J.: Prentice-Hall, 1960.

Hogan, W. P. "Multinational Firms, Labour Utilization and Trade Flows." *Journal of Industrial Relations* (Sydney) 14 (September 1972): 225–37.

Hughes, B., and Schwarz, J. "Dimensions of Political Integration and the Experience of the EEC." *International Studies Quarterly* 16, no. 3 (September 1972): 263–94.

*Industrial Democracy.* Report by the TUC General Council to the 1974 Trade Union Congress, London, England.

International Confederation of Free Trade Unions. *The Multinational Challenge.* Conference Reports no. 2. Brussels, Belgium, September 1971.

International Federation of Commercial, Clerical and Technical Employees. "Facing Multinationals—The Strategy of FIET," 17 OC/11/6. Internal, confidential document. Geneva, Switzerland, 1973.

International Federation of Musicians. *Report on the Activity,* Seventh Business Period, Autumn 1969–Autumn 1972, London.

International Labor Organization. *Multinational Enterprises and Social Policy.* Geneva, 1973. (ITS: Studies and reports. New series, 79).

————. *The Relationship Between Multinational Corporations and Social Policy.* Geneva, Switzerland, 1972.

International Metalworkers Federation. *IMF Systematic Analysis of Multinational Companies Worldwide and at the Subsidiary Level, I. The Ford Motor Company.* Geneva, Switzerland, October 1974.

Jacobs, Eric. *European Trade Unionism.* New York: Holmes and Meier, 1973.

Johnson, Harry. "The Efficiency and Welfare Implications of the International Corporation." In *The International Corporation.* Edited by Charles P. Kindleberger. Cambridge, Mass.: MIT Press, 1970.

Judd, Frank. "Third World and the Multinationals." *Third World* (London) 2 (February 1973): 5–9.

Kaplan, Morton. *System and Process in International Politics.* New York: Wiley, 1957.

Kapoor, Ashok, and Brub, P. D., eds. *The Multinational Enterprise in Transition: Selected Readings and Essays.* Princeton, N.J.: Darwin Press, 1972.

Kassalow, Everett M. "The International Metalworkers Federation and the Multinational Automobile Companies." Unpublished manuscript. Madison: University of Wisconsin, March 1974.

Kelman, Herbert C. *International Behavior: A Social-Psychological Analysis.* For the Society for the Psychological Study of Social Issues. New York: Holt, Rinehart and Winston, 1965.

Keohane, Robert O., and Nye, Joseph S., eds. "Transnational Relations and World Politics." *International Organization* 25 (Summer 1971): 329–758.

Kindleberger, Charles. *American Business Abroad: Six Lectures on Direct Investments.* New Haven, Conn.: Yale University Press, 1969.

Krause, Lawrence B. "The International Economic System and the Multinational Corporation." *Annals of the American Academy of Political and Social Science* 403 (September 1972): 93–103.

Kujawa, Duane. *International Labor Relations Management in the Automobile Industry: A Comparative Study of Chrysler, Ford and General Motors.* New York: Praeger, 1971.

Landelius, Torsten. *Workers, Employers and Governments: A Comparative Study of Delegations and Groups at the International Labor Conference, 1919–1964.* Stockholm: Norstedt and Soner, 1965.

Lea, D. "Multinational Companies and Trade Union Interests." In *The Multinational Enterprise.* Edited by J. H. Dunning. New York: Praeger, 1971.

Lenin, V. I. *Imperialism, The Highest Stage of Capitalism.* New York: International Publishers, 1939.

Levinson, Charles. *Industry's Democratic Revolution.* London: Allen & Unwin, 1974.

———. *International Trade Unionism.* London: Allen & Unwin, 1972.

Lindberg, L. *The Political Dynamics of European Economic Integration.* Stanford, Calif.: Stanford University Press, 1963.

Lindberg, L., and Scheingold, S. A. *Regional Integration: Theory and Research.* Cambridge, Mass.: Harvard University Press, 1971.

———. *Europe's Would-Be Polity.* Englewood Cliffs, N.J.: Prentice-Hall, 1970.

Lovell, Enid Baird. "Multinational Corporations and the Nation-State." *Journal of World Trade Law* (London) 7 (May-June 1973): 267–92.

———. *Nationalism or Interdependence: The Alternatives. International Survey of Business Option and Experience.* New York: National Industrial Conference Board, 1969.

Marx, Eli, and Kendall, Walter. *Unions in Europe.* Brighton, England: Center for Contemporary European Studies, University of Sussex, 1971.

Marx, Karl, and Engels, Friedrich. *The Communist Manifesto.* Edited by S. H. Beer. New York: Appleton Century Crofts, 1955.

Mitrany, David. *A Working Peace System.* Chicago: Quadrangle Books, 1966.

Modelski, G. "Multinational Business. A Global Perspective." *International Studies Quarterly* 16 (December 1972): 407–32.

————. "The Corporation in World Society." In *Yearbook of World Affairs,* vol. 22. London: Stevens and Sons, 1968.

Niblock, M. *The EEC: National Parliaments in Community Decision-Making.* London: Chatham House, 1971.

Northrup, H., and Rowan, R. "Multinational Collective Bargaining Activity: The Factual Record in Chemicals, Glass, and Rubber Tires. Pt. II." *Columbia Journal of World Business* 9 (Summer 1974): 49–63.

Nye, Joseph S. "Multinational Enterprises and Prospects for Regional and Global Political Integration." *Annals of the American Academy of Political and Social Science* 403 (September 1972): 116–26.

————, ed. *International Regionalism: Readings.* Under the auspices of the Center for International Affairs, Harvard University. Boston: Little, Brown, 1968.

Organization for Economic Cooperation and Development. Regional Joint Seminar on Prospects for Labor/Management Cooperation in the Enterprise. 1972.

————. Labor Problems in Multinational Firms: Report on a Meeting of Management Experts. Paris: Manpower and Social Affairs Directorate, October 9, 1972.

————. Report on the Meeting of Trade Union Experts on Multinational Companies, Paris, MAS (69) 23, 23, July 1970.

Osterberg, David, and Fouad, Ajami. "The Multinational Corporation: Expanding the Frontiers of World Politics." *Journal of Conflict Resolution* 15 (December 1971): 457–70.

Paquet, Gilles, ed. *The Multinational Firm and the Nation-State.* Don Mills, Ontario: Collier Macmillan Canada, 1972.

Perlmutter, Howard V. "The Multinational Firm and the Future." *Annals of the American Academy of Political and Social Science* 403 (September 1972): 139–52.

————. "Towards Research on and Development of Nations, Unions and Firms as Worldwide Institutions." *International Studies of Management and Organization* 1 (Winter 1971–72):419–49.

Polites, George. "Multinational Corporations: The Employers' View." *Journal of Industrial Relations* (Sydney) 15 (March 1973): 64–74.

Puchala, Donald. "The Pattern of Contemporary Regional Integration." *International Studies Quarterly* 12, no. 1 (March 1968): 38–64.

Pye, Lucian W., and Sidney Verba, eds. *Political Culture and Political Development.* Princeton, N.J.: Princeton University Press, 1965.

Rajh, Zdenko. "Multinational Companies: Tendencies Toward Capital Integration and the Interests of the Working Class." *Review of International Affairs* (Belgrade) 23 (July 1972): 26–28.

Roberts, B. C. "Multinational Collective Bargaining: A European Prospect?" *British Journal of Industrial Relations* 11, no. 1 (March 1973).

Roberts, E. *Workers Control.* London: Allen & Unwin, 1973.

Robinson, Richard D. "The Developing Countries, Development and the Multinational Corporation." *Annals of the American Academy of Political and Social Science* 403 (September 1972): 67–70.

Rogers, Paolo N. "Multinational Corporations: A European View." *Annals of the American Academy of Political and Social Science* 403 (September 1972): 58–66.

Rolfe, Sidney E. *The Multinational Corporation.* New York: Foreign Policy Association, 1970.

Rosecrance, Richard. *Action and Reaction in World Politics.* Boston: Little, Brown, 1963.

Rubin, Seymour J. "Multinational Enterprise and National Sovereignty: A Skeptic's Analysis." *Law and Policy in International Business* 3, no. 1 (1971): 1–41.

Russet, Bruce M. *International Regions and the International System: A Study in Political Ecology.* Series in Comparative Government and International Politics. Chicago: Rand McNally, 1967.

Scheingold, S. *The Rule of Law in European Integration: The Rule of the Schuman Plan.* New Haven, Conn.: Yale University Press, 1965.

Segal, Ronald. "Multinational Corporations: Everywhere at Home, Home Nowhere." *Center (for the Study of Democratic Institutions) Magazine* 6 (May–June 1973): 8–14.

Shaker, Frank. "The Multinational Corporation: The New Imperialism?" *Columbia Journal of World Business* 5 (November-December 1970): 80–84.

Siemens, Peter von. "Les Societes Multinationales—Pionniers de l'Integration Economique Mondiale." *Revue de la Societe d'Etudes et d'Expansion* (Liege), no. 253 (November–December 1972): 890–97.

Singer, J. D., ed. *Human Behavior and International Politics.* Chicago: Rand McNally, 1965.

Souhami, Gerard. "Societes Multinationales, Gouvernments Nationaux et Organisations Supranationales." *Revue du Marche Commun* (Paris), no. 163 (March 1973): 111–13.

———. "The Multinational Corporation: Measuring the Consequences." *Columbia Journal of World Business* 6 (January–February 1971): 59–64.

Stephenson, H. *The Coming Clash—The Impact of Multinational Corporations on National States.* New York: Saturday Press Review, 1972.

Stobaugh, Robert B. "U.S. Multinational Enterprises and the U.S. Economy." In *The Multinational Corporation.* vol. 1 (Washington, D.C.: U.S. Department of Commerce, March 1972).

*Symposium of International Collective Bargaining, Geneva, 1969.* Edited by H. Gunter. London: Macmillan, 1972.

"Symposium with Michele Sindona on the Role of Multinational Corporations." *Columbia Journal of World Business* 8 (Summer 1973): 43–48.

Trades Union Congress. *International Companies.* London: Congress House, October 21, 1970.

Trezise, Philip H. "Some Policy Implications of the Multinational Corporation." *Department of State (United States) Bulletin* 64 (May 24, 1971): 669–72.

Troeller, Ruth R. "Multinational Corporations in a Changing Europe." *Journal of World Trade Law* 7 (May-June 1973): 293–300.

Tugendhat, Christopher. *The Multinationals.* Middlesex, England: Penguin Books, 1973.

———. *The Multinationals.* London: Eyre and Spottiswoode, 1971.

Turner, Louis. *Invisible Empires: Multinational Companies and the Modern World*. London: Hamish Hamilton, 1970.

Tyler, Gus. "Multinationals: A Global Menace." *Atlantic Community Quarterly* 10 (Winter 1972–1973): 512–26.

United Nations. Department of Economic and Social Affairs. *Multinational Corporations in World Development* (ST/ECA/190), 1973.

U.S., Congress. Senate. Committee on Finance. *The Multinational Corporation and the World Economy*. 93rd Cong., 1st sess., 1973.

———. Senate. Committee on Finance. *Multinational Corporations: a compendium of papers*. 93rd Cong., 1st sess., 1973.

———. Senate. Committee on Finance. *Multinational Corporations: Hearings before the subcommittee*. 93rd Cong., 1st sess., February 26, 28 and March 1, 6, 1973.

———. Senate. Tariff Commission. *Implications of Multinational Firms for World Trade and Investment and for U.S.Trade and Labor*. 93rd Cong., 1st sess., 1978.

Vernon, Raymond. "Influence of National Origins on the Strategy of Multinational Enterprise." *Revue Economique* (Paris) 23 (July 1972): 547–62.

———. *Multinational Enterprise and National Security*. Adelphi Papers no. 74. London, 1971.

———. *Sovereignty at Bay: The Multinational Spread of U.S. Enterprises*. Harvard Multinational Enterprise Series. New York: Basic Books, 1971.

———. "Conflict and Resolution Between Foreign Direct Investors and Less Developed Countries." *Public Policy* 17 (Fall 1968): 333–51.

———. "The Multinational Corporation." *Atlantic Community Quarterly* 5 (Winter 1967–1968): 533–39.

Walker, Kenneth F. "Labor Problems in Multinational Firms: A Report on a Meeting of Management Experts, Paris, June 21–23, 1972." Paris: Organization for Economic Cooperation and Development, 1972.

Warner, Malcolm, and Louis Turner. "Trade Unions and the Multi-National Firm." *Journal of Industrial Relations* (Sydney) 14 (June 1972): 143–69.

Willatt, Norris. *Multinational Unions*. London: Financial Times, 1974.

Windmuller, John P. "International Trade Union Organizations: Structures, Functions, Limitations." In *International Labor.* Edited by Solomon Barkin. New York: Harper & Row, 1967.

World Federation of Labor. "For a Policy to Cope with Multinational Companies." Extracts from the World Confederation of Labor Congress, September 1973.

# ABOUT THE AUTHOR

PAUL WEINBERG is Vice President–Employee Relations for a major multinational corporation. Prior to this he served in a number of personnel and labor relations capacities with large companies and as a consultant. He is an expert on U.S. and international labor matters and has represented the United States government at the International Labor Organization on the issue of workers participation in management.

Dr. Weinberg received his Ph.D. from New York University—Department of Political Science. He also holds an M.A. from McGill University with a specialty in political theory and international relations and a B.S. from Cornell University's School of Industrial and Labor Relations.

In addition to a number of journal articles which he has written, Dr. Weinberg has edited *Emerging Sectors of Collective Bargaining* and *Human Values and Technological Change*, both published by McGill University Industrial Relations Center.

# RELATED TITLES
## published by
## Praeger Special Studies

INTERNATIONAL LABOR AND THE MULTINATIONAL ENTER-PRISE
edited by Duane Kujawa

*WORKER MILITANCY AND ITS CONSEQUENCES, 1965–75:
New Directions in Western Industrial Relations
edited by Solomon Barkin

WORKER SELF-MANAGEMENT IN INDUSTRY:
The West European Experience
edited by G. David Garson

---

*Also available in paperback.